Living Words

Sh'ma שמע

Since 1970, *Sh'ma* has served as a gathering place for independent voices eager to be heard across the Jewish religious, social and political landscape. Through our diversity, intensity, frequency and constancy, we have served as a public diary of the North American Jewish experience. In the pages of *Sh'ma*, we discuss topics that cut to the very core of our Jewish sense of self. Our tactic is dialogue — rich conversation of differing positions presented in an honest, respectful, and purposeful way. We seek to bring all of our readers to the table of sacred conversation. We cover topics as diverse as the politics of gender; trends in new Jewish social and political involvement; questions of culture and personal identity; ritual innovations; and new readings of ancient texts. Our readers are like our authors: sharp, seeking, concerned, and caring.

Share your voice in dialogue on Sh`ma's Website: *www.Shma.com*

Living Words

Best High Holiday Sermons of 5759
Foreword by Rabbi Nina Beth Cardin

Sh'ma שמע

Library of Congress Cataloging-in-Publication Data
Sh'ma
Living Words: Best High Holiday Sermons of 5759
ISBN 0-9664306-1-1

10 9 8 7 6 5 4 3 2 1

Contents

v

Acknowledgments

Gathering any collection of writings is a task both arduous and inspiring. The role of Editor, much like that of a mother, is as an enabler, helping to cultivate and clarify the voices of the writers. Gathering and coordinating efforts on behalf of this collection of High Holiday sermons has been the task of Dinah Zeltser, an intern from the Hornstein Program in Jewish Communal Service at Brandeis University. She has lent her imagination and considerable skill to the project. I would also like to acknowledge Natasha Shabat, who has edited, designed, and typeset the book; Jesse Kahn, the creative artist behind the book's cover; and my colleagues in the Jewish Family & Life! office who have lent their ears and eyes and hands to this project: Gabi Soble, Joshua Pines, Ronnie Friedland, Jennifer Shulman, Hyung Park, Janna Rogat, and Judith Bolton-Fasman. More specifically, I want to thank Yosef I. Abramowitz, the publisher of *Sh'ma*, whose courage, sensibilities, and generosity inspire us all.

Rabbi Eugene Borowitz, the founding Editor of *Sh'ma*, has provided the journal with his vision and blessed it with a profound moral and journalistic responsibility, which I humbly accept and hope to meet. Throughout the journal's travels, *Sh'ma* has had the good fortune to be guided by a dedicated, intellectual cadre of Jewish leaders, most recently Rabbi Nina Beth Cardin. Her wisdom and devotion to the journal are immeasurable. She currently chairs the Advisory Committee, which also includes Caroline Harris, Susan Laden, Carl Sheingold, and Larry Yudelson.

For 28 years, *Sh'ma* has built a community of readers among the intellectual, spiritual, cultural and communal leadership of North America. The pages of *Sh'ma* have been filled with essays that have inspired social change and enlarged the table at which Jews sit with each other in dialogue. Maintaining this community of readers and writers is a challenge and a source of great satisfaction. To you, our readers, we offer this collection of sermons. We hope they will inspire, teach, and prepare you for the High Holy Days.

Susan Berrin
Editor
June, 1999
Sivan, 5759

Foreword

For the rabbi, the High Holiday sermon is a return to Sinai. The audience is never so big; the hearts never so open; the atmosphere never so charged; and the stakes never so high as on these days of repentance. If political discretion and a dash of diffidence are necessary other days of the year, they can be cast aside now. This is the time for the rabbi to be like Joshua — taking the words of God given by Moses and prodding and guiding and goading the Jews to the promised land. The rabbi is emboldened on these rare days of communal introspection to show the passion that can ignite their spirits and bind their wounded hearts. The rabbi seeks to stake a claim, lead the flock, lay the groundwork for the personal and congregational dreams for the coming year. This is the time for the rabbi to ascend that pulpit and fill it.

Not all in one talk. The High Holidays offer the opportunity for six sermons: two a day for three days. Pacing is an issue. The rabbi considers, What shall I talk about? Shall I join the sermons in a common theme? Is this too limiting? What news items are dominating the world's attention and demand my response?

Around June or July, every conversation, every news article, every book the rabbi encounters is filtered through the query, "Would this make a good High Holiday sermon?" There is a lot of writing to be done, a lot of stories to be found and reworked, a lot of reawakening to do. The rabbi's own days become spiritually heightened as the markers of holiness in the world are once again allowed to stand in high relief. For rabbis, the High Holidays come early every year.

Choosing sermon topics is only the first task. Once that is done, their arrangement must be decided. How will they sit next to the others? What is the flow of the various messages? Will they fit well together to offer a guide to this year's behavior? Each one serves as a frame for the other, like delicate shells arrayed on a shelf, playing off the hue cast by the other. Yet the intrinsic aesthetics of the placement of the sermon must be weighed against a cruder measure: audience share. The congregation on the first day of Rosh Hashanah is often larger than the second. But which is the fuller service — night or day? Which talk is shaping up better? Which shall be the introduction? Shall I save political/social topics for daytime? Spiritual ones for the evening? The other way around? The rabbi must be impresario and programmer as well as preacher.

For the listener, the High Holiday sermon is an opportunity to rummage around in the rabbi's psyche. Why did s/he choose that topic this year? What metaphors does s/he employ and what does that mean? Is this topic an issue that bothers the rabbi personally, or is it an issue that s/he thinks ought to bother me? There is a tug of war: Who is this sermon about? Me or the rabbi? All sermons start out being about the rabbi — how entertaining s/he is, how clever, how on-target, how true. But the successful sermon subtly shifts the listeners' focus so the thoughts are no longer on the rabbi's performance, but on the rabbi's message. And it does not stop there. There is another consciousness shift, from the rabbi's message to the listener's own life. A sermon that satisfies both rabbi and listener gives the listener hope, strength, confidence, a sense of renewal and a sense of belonging.

In this book, we have gathered some of the finest sermons of 5759 (1998) that carry the listener across that consciousness threshold. Each sermon is a full message. It stands on its own, and fills its plate. But it is also a partner to others in its cluster. Reading it, then, is like eating only one course of a six-course meal. No one sermon reveals the fullness of the repast the rabbi has prepared.

In addition, you will be reading text that was committed to writing for the purpose of being spoken. The best sermons have an aural component to them as well as a conceptual one. Reading bits and pieces aloud is highly recommended.

The sermons here present a broad swath of topics, from the timely to the timeless: our role in building better schools for America; the value and the methods of forgiveness; Jewish unity; personal responsibility and responsiveness; remembering; opening up the way into Judaism and Jewish practice, and more. The tones were personal, analytical, humorous, subdued. In the demography of the authorship, they provide insights into the changing ways, customs, and concerns of the American Jew. They, more than anything else, comprise the spiritual diary of the American Jew.

We hope that this is *Sh'ma*'s first in a series of collections of High Holiday sermons. Over the years and decades, when seen as a whole, the series will serve as an invaluable witness to the development, dreams, and desires of this dynamic, changing Jewish people.

Nina Beth Cardin
Chair, *Sh'ma* Advisory Committee

It's All How You Look at It

Shoshana Gelfand

---

*It is entirely possible not to have physical
eyesight, while still being capable of
incredible insights and visions.*

There is a beautiful story about a king who had a most unusual diamond. It was quite remarkable, perfect in every way. He liked to take it out and watch it sparkle in the light. And when he was done admiring it, he always took great pains to place it carefully back in its case so it would not get scratched. One day, however, when he took out the diamond to admire it, he discovered to his horror that there was a hairline crack running right down the middle. He was devastated. His perfect diamond — ruined. The king became very depressed. He refused to see or talk to anyone. Finally, his advisors realized that something had to be done. So they put out a call across the land, proclaiming that whoever could fix the king's diamond would be handsomely rewarded. But no one stepped forward to answer the call. No one could figure out how to fix a cracked diamond.

Then a woman appeared at the castle and said she knew much about diamonds; but she would need to take it to her workshop for a year. Figuring they had nothing to lose, the king's advisors sent her away with the diamond. A year later, she reappeared and insisted on personally returning the diamond to the king. Hopeful that perhaps she had indeed fixed his diamond, the king emerged from his chambers for the first time since the crack had appeared. She handed the diamond back to him. The king looked at it and then let out a yell of rage, "You didn't fix my diamond! Look, the crack is still there!" The woman calmly replied, "Where? I don't see any crack." The king pointed to where the hairline crack still did indeed exist. But the woman responded, "Oh that! That, your majesty, is not a crack. That is the stem of a rose. If you look carefully, you will see that I have spent the last year carving the petals of the rose onto the diamond." The king looked back at the diamond, and only then did he see the most beautiful rose he could ever have imagined. His flawed diamond, he realized, was even more perfect than before.

In this story, the king takes life at face value. If there appears to be a crack in the diamond, the king accepts that and responds by becoming a recluse. The woman, on the other hand, is able to see beyond the obvious. She has the vision to take a seemingly difficult situation and transform it into a thing of beauty. So much of the time, when we are down, we feel like following the king's example. It's the easy way out. It is so much more difficult to try and look at the situation from various angles — to try and find alternate options.

In this morning's Torah portion, we encounter two characters who went through a difficult experience together. The *Akedah*, the binding of Yitzhak, was traumatic for both Avraham and Yitzhak. Yet their responses in the end differ greatly. Avraham manages to keep his ability to see various options and to continue with life; Yitzhak, on the other hand, does not seem to be able to develop this same sense of vision. So the question for us is: What message is the *Akedah* trying to teach us about vision? Let us take a few moments to examine the text together. Note carefully when and how the Torah uses the metaphor of sight in this story.

Our Torah portion begins in Genesis, Chapter 22, by telling us that God tested Avraham. While certainly this is true, it is clearly not the whole truth. Avraham wasn't the only one being tested. There are *midrashim* that claim Yitzhak was 37 years old at the time of the *Akedah*. Others say age 13. Either way, this is old enough for Yitzhak to be aware of his actions and their implications. It seems that both father and son were being tested — tested to see how each one would handle the unimaginable.

God tells Avraham: "Take now your son, your only son, whom you love, Yitzhak, and go to the Land of

Moriah; and offer him there as a sacrifice on one of the mountains which I will tell you." *Moriah* means "vision." So God is telling Avraham to take Yitzhak to the "Land of Vision."

The two set off with their entourage. On the third day, Avraham *lifted his eyes* and *saw* the place where the sacrifice was to take place. Notice how Avraham is able to raise his eyes and know that the mountain he sees is the predetermined place. Avraham has a sense of vision. Avraham is able to look at something and not just see it literally, but understand its significance.

Once they arrive at the mountain, Avraham and Yitzhak leave their servants and ascend together. The Torah explicitly mentions that they went up together. The test is for both of them. They are in it together. At one point, Yitzhak calls out to his father, asking where the lamb is for the sacrifice. Avraham's answer is telling: "God will see to the sheep for His burnt offering, my son." "God will see" — again, Avraham is the one who understands vision. Yitzhak is totally in the dark. He did not "see" the mountain and now he cannot understand that God will "see to" the sheep.

Finally, Yitzhak is bound on the altar. Avraham is ready to sacrifice him when an angel calls out and stops him from going through with the act. At this point, God seems satisfied that Avraham was indeed willing to sacrifice his son; there is no need to carry through with the action. One might think this to be a good place to end the story. But here is actually where the real test begins, for the real test is whether Avraham and Yitzhak can continue affirming life even after having experienced such a traumatic event. Will they have the vision to make their world meaningful? Or will they retreat into themselves like the king whose diamond was cracked?

We soon find out that Avraham does manage to keep his sense of vision. In fact, the very next action in the story says, "Avraham lifted up his eyes and looked and behold, behind him there was a ram, caught in the thicket by its horns." So Avraham sacrifices the ram in place of Yitzhak. Avraham can still see. He is able to envision alternate options. Thus, instead of sacrificing his son, he sacrifices the ram. Had Avraham not been able to envision options, he would not have seen the ram. Or if he did see it, it would not have occurred to him to sacrifice it in place of his son. The final clincher of the *Akedah* story reads, "And Avraham called the name of that place *Adonai-yireh*; as it is said to this day: 'In the mount where the Lord appeared,.''

We can see from the fact that Avraham chooses to name the place "*Adonai-yireh*" that this story is indeed about vision, about being able to reconstruct one's world even when it appears to be falling apart. How easy it would have been for Avraham to say, "Forget this, I cannot deal with a God who demands this kind of faith." But Avraham has vision. Avraham is able to take the trauma of the *Akedah* and learn and grow from it. After the *Akedah*, we see Avraham actively involved with his family. He buries his wife, Sarah. He goes to great pains to find the correct wife for Yitzhak. And he even goes on to remarry and have six more children before he dies. Despite whatever horrors Avraham endured as the result of the *Akedah*, he did not shirk his responsibility to his family. Nor did he allow his life to come to a standstill.

But what about Yitzhak? Where is he during all of this? He seems to have disappeared — literally out of sight. The last we saw of him was when the angel stopped the sacrifice before it could begin. What happened to him after that? It is difficult to know because the Torah is silent on this matter. What makes the question even more acute is that the Torah explicitly tells us that Avraham returned to his servants at the foot of the mountain. But the verb is in the singular. It would seem that Yitzhak was not with him.

So, I ask again, where is Yitzhak? The biblical commentators have much to say about this exact question. Some *midrashim* claim that, like any good Jewish boy, he went off to study in *yeshiva* until it was time to get married. The Torah, however, gives no indication of this. If we follow the text faithfully, then the next time we see Yitzhak is when he marries Rivkah. The marriage, as I noted, was orchestrated primarily by Avraham, not Yitzhak. Yitzhak still acts as a passive child, traumatized by the *Akedah* and mourning for his dead mother. Only after he marries Rivkah is Yitzhak comforted over the loss of his mother.

Finally, we encounter Yitzhak in his only adult role in the Torah. He and Rivkah have had two children — Yaakov and Esav. Esav sells his birthright to Yaakov in exchange for a bowl of lentil soup. Then Yaakov decides to steal Esav's blessing as well as his birthright. You may recall that Yaakov succeeds in this ploy. It seems that Yitzhak cannot tell the difference between his own children. How odd. But if we look at the opening to this story, we have a clue as to why Yitzhak cannot tell the difference. The story begins with the words, "Yitzhak's eyes were dim." He couldn't see well. But let me suggest that the Torah here is not talking about mere physical sight. The Torah, rather, is referring to the ability to see the larger picture. It is entirely possible not to have physical eyesight, while still being capable of incredible insights and visions. But we are not talking about Yitzhak's physical vision here. We are talking about his ability to function in the world.

"Yitzhak's eyes were dim." Yitzhak could not see. Yitzhak did not have vision. What happened to Yitzhak's vision? Why couldn't he see like his father Avraham? If we go back to the story of the *Akedah*, we find that after the near disaster of sacrifice, Avraham looks up and sees the ram. Yitzhak, it seems, does not look up. Both men have experienced a terrible moment in time, but Yitzhak does not look up afterwards. He withdraws. He does not make an effort to move on. He does not take control of his life. For this reason, he fails to see the ram. He fails to see at all. And in the end, he becomes spiritually blind and incapable of functioning and participating in the world around him.

Judaism does not see the world through rose-colored glasses. It is not oblivious to the pain and struggles we face in our lives. It is not oblivious to the pain that father and son endured as part of going through the *Akedah*. The ultimate question, however, is how can we, like Avraham, make our lives spiritually significant even in the face of overwhelming trials?

Part of the answer lies in the prayers of the High Holiday service. On both Rosh Hashanah and Yom Kippur we recite the prayer, *Unetaneh Tokef*, usually noted because of its terrifying passage about who will live and who will die, and how each one will die. For a Jew, however, it is the last line which is the most important: *U'teshuvah u'tefillah u'tzedakah ma'avirin et ro'ah ha-g'zerah*: "But repentance, prayer, and righteousness avert the severity of the decree." Unfortunately, many *mahzorim* translate the passage incorrectly, as "avert the severe decree." It may sound like a minor detail, but there is a world of difference between these two statements. To say that these actions can avert the severe decree implies that somehow we can change the hand we are dealt if only we have enough piety. This is simply not true. Not every sickness can be cured. Not every marriage can be saved. Not every loved one can be spared death.

What is crucial to understand is that the actions we choose to take in the face of adversity can make a difference in our lives. They can avert the severity of the decree, not the decree itself. Our actions can allow us to do the best we can with whatever we have to work with. We may not be able to change the objective reality, but we do have the ability — like Avraham — to transform meaninglessness into meaning, and the profane into the sacred.

May we all have a year of blessing and peace, despite the many problems that face us.

May we try to look up from our troubles and find alternate perspectives.

And may we use our vision to transform our flawed diamonds into objects of beauty.

Rabbi Shoshana Gelfand is the director of Programs at the Wexner Heritage Foundation. She is a Conservative rabbi, ordained at the Jewish Theological Seminary in 1993, where she studied as a Wexner Fellow. She graduated magna cum laude from Bryn Mawr College and was a MacCracken Fellow at New York University, where she has done graduate work toward a doctoral degree in Talmud.
Rabbi Gelfand served for two years as the Assistant Rabbi at Congregation Anshe Emet in Chicago, IL, and for one year as Scholar-in-Residence at the Jewish Community Center of Staten Island, NY. She has also served as Associate Scholar-in-Residence at Brandeis-Bardin in California. Rabbi Gelfand has published in The Journal of Synagogue Music *and* Masoret *and she is a contributing editor to* The Jewish Spectator. *She currently serves on the boards of The Institute for Contemporary Midrash and Project Kesher — an organization that teaches Judaism to women in the Former Soviet Union. She is beginning to work with Camp Ramah Darom to create a Center for Southern Jewry near Atlanta, GA.*

Writing Your Eulogy

Michael Gold

---

*Other traditions speak of the pleasures of
the next world; Judaism asks, Did you
really enjoy this world?*

A woman called the newspaper when her husband died. She wanted to place an obituary for her husband. "That is fine, but we do charge by the word," said the newspaper. "If that is so, then just write 'Schwartz Died.'" The newspaper responded, "Madam, there is a five-word minimum." "OK," said the woman, "Write, 'Schwartz Died, Cadillac for Sale.'"

That sounds like a eulogy for people I have met. They will be remembered chiefly for the things they leave behind. To quote a famous bumper sticker, "Whoever dies with the most toys wins." Today, as we prepare to say *Yizkor* prayers for those no longer with us, I want to speak about obituaries and eulogies. I want to ask, How will you be remembered? Will your last legacy be "Cadillac for sale, Lexus available, golf clubs, tennis racket, things"? Or will it be something more?

As I mentioned when the High Holidays began, Rosh Hashana is about birth and Yom Kippur is about death. On Rosh Hashana we remember our birth, our parents' dreams and hopes for us. And on Yom Kippur we relive our deaths. We are forced to confront what is truly important in our lives.

Just as the Torah reading on Rosh Hashana spoke of the birth of Isaac, the Torah reading today speaks of the deaths of Aaron's two sons. Throughout the day we relive our own deaths. We wear white, just as a body is dressed in a white shroud. (Incidentally, by Jewish law, we do not dress our loved ones in their best suits. Burial in an Armani suit is not the Jewish way. We dress them in simple white linen garments called *tachrichim*, shrouds, without pockets because we cannot take possessions with us.)

Rabbi Yitz Greenberg, one of the foremost teachers in our nation, taught that on Yom Kippur we live as spiritual beings. We do not eat, we do not drink, we do not wash, we do not wear comfortable shoes nor anoint ourselves with perfume or cologne, we do not enjoy sexual relations, we do not work. All the physical things that make us human are set aside. We confront our maker with words like "As clay we are, that forms beneath the hands of our Maker." Like death, we are not in control. For no man or woman knows the day of his or her death. As spiritual beings we face God.

On Yom Kippur, we speak about who shall live and who shall die. On Rosh Hashana it may be written, but today our fate will be sealed. Will this be the year that we leave this world to face our Maker? Then, at the height of our Yom Kippur prayers, when the synagogue is filled with worshippers, we recite *yizkor*, prayers for those who have gone before us. Even as we recite these prayers, we confront our own deaths. Why? Why do we Jews gather once a year and relive our own deaths?

I received an answer this year. I went to the hospital to visit a young man who had been in an extremely serious auto accident. He was badly injured and would need several months of serious rehabilitation. Fortunately, he would fully recover. The person in the other car was not so lucky. She died in the accident.

I spoke to the man as he lay in his hospital bed. Although he could not remember the details of the accident, he knew that he had had a brush with death. He told me of his resolution to make some major changes in his life. Too much time had been spent partying, drinking, going in the wrong direction. No more. He had survived, and he was going to turn his life around. As I prayed with him and encouraged him, I realized that there is nothing like a brush with death to make us rethink our priorities. That is why the rabbis say, "Repent one day before you die."

On Yom Kippur we contemplate our deaths because it helps us to focus. It is like reliving that accident without, thank God, the hospital stay. On Yom

Kippur we look at our lives and ask, what will our obituaries be like? How will we be eulogized?

I once heard a motivational speaker give the following talk. He said, "Imagine your own funeral. You are laid out in your best clothes. [He was a Christian, and did not realize that Jews dress in shrouds.] Imagine all your family and friends walking by, tears being shed as they see you at rest. [Of course, at Jewish funerals, we do not have public viewings. It is considered disrespectful.] Then the service begins, and four people get up to eulogize you.

"The first speaker is a co-worker from your place of business. He or she talks about you in the world of work. Were you honest? Were you kind, not just to your boss and your clients, but to your subordinates and your co-workers? What kind of reputation did you have in the world of business? Did people enjoy doing business with you? Did they trust you?

"The second speaker is a neighbor. What kind of neighbor were you? Did you greet people with a smile when you saw them on the street? Could people count on you? Did you have friends? Were you open and honest with people? When others were in need, were you there with a helping hand?

"The third speaker is a member of your family, perhaps one of your children or grandchildren. They remember you as a husband or wife, father or mother, grandfather or grandmother, brother or sister. Were you there for your family? Did you care? Did you love them unconditionally? Did you set standards for your children? Did you have a marriage that was blessed? Did you put as much energy into your family as you did into your business?

The motivational speaker continued, "Finally the fourth speaker is your clergy, your priest, minister, or rabbi. How would they sum up your life? Did you love God, and live a life that would make God proud? Did you love your neighbor? Did you fulfill your mission on this earth?"

Nothing focuses the mind like contemplating our own eulogy. I often think about the motivational speaker's words. As a rabbi, I am often called upon to give eulogies, sometimes for people I knew and cared deeply about, too often for strangers who never darkened the door of a synagogue. My teacher in practical rabbinics, Rabbi Bill Horn of Summit, New Jersey, taught me always to look for something good in people's lives, some *mitzvah* they did, some gift they gave the world. We can always learn from someone's life.

I remember Rabbi Horn sharing a story with our class. Two sons had asked him to bury their father. When he tried to get information for the eulogy, the sons said, "Our father was a no-goodnik who never did a decent thing in his life. The best thing he ever did for us was to die." How do you write a eulogy on that information? Rabbi Horn began his eulogy, "Here was a man whose last act was for his children."

What should our eulogies be like?

On Yom Kippur we consider our own deaths. Yom Kippur is an opportunity to write our own eulogies, to think about how we will be remembered. I want to share with you on this Yom Kippur day a series of teachings from Jewish tradition. Judaism teaches that when we are called to the next world we will be asked a series of questions. Let me share five of those questions with you today.

The first is from the Jerusalem Talmud: *Atid adam liten din vecheshbon al kol shera'ita einav velo achal.* "In the future each of us must give an accounting for every legitimate pleasure we saw but did not enjoy." (*Jer. Kiddushin 4:12*) What a powerful statement. Life is to be savored and enjoyed. When John Maynard Keynes, the famous economist, was on his deathbed, people asked him "Lord Keynes, do you have any regrets?" "Yes," he replied, "I should have tasted more champagne."

Judaism is filled with things we are not allowed to do. There are limitations on what we eat, what we drink, who we have sex with, who we marry, what we do on certain days of the week and dates of the year. Judaism tries to instill within us a sense of self-discipline and holiness. Still, within Jewish tradition there is so much to be enjoyed. Other religious traditions speak of asceticism as the path to holiness, living in a monastery, taking vows of abstinence, celibacy, poverty. That has never been the Jewish way to God.

Judaism says, Enjoy life. The book of Ecclesiastes reads "Go thy way, eat thy bread with joy and drink thy wine with merry heart... let thy garments be always white and let thy head lack no oil. Enjoy life with the wife whom thou lovest..." (*Ecc. 9:7–9*). Other traditions may speak of the pleasures of the next world; Judaism asks, Did you really enjoy this world?

The Babylonian Talmud asks four other questions: *Amar rava, besha'ah shemachnisim adam ledin omrim lo...* "Rava taught, at the time when a man goes for his final judgment, they say to him..." *Nasata natata be'emunah?* "Did you give and take with faithfulness?" *(Shabbat 31a)* Were you honest in your business dealings? Ultimately, we do not take our possessions to the next world, but we do take our good name. No one is interested if we did well. They are only interested if we did good.

There is a classical Hasidic story. A rabbi, a great scholar and sage, filled his whole life with acts of piety. He knew that he would be justly rewarded in the world to come. So he prayed to God to let him see who would sit next to him in the next world, who would be his study partner? And God granted him his wish.

God took him to a little shop where a poor shoemaker slaved away. All day and far into the night the man made shoes, and yet he seemed to have little to show for it. The shop was poor. The man never took time to study, he badly needed to bathe and change clothes. The rabbi was outraged. "O God, after all my acts of piety, this man is to be my neighbor and study partner! What kind of justice is this?" God answered, "Go talk to the shoe maker."

The rabbi introduced himself. The shoemaker answered, "I have heard of your great piety. I wish I had time to learn with you. But who has the time. All day I work hard to make shoes for the rich; they pay my living. And then, when there is leather left over, all night I work hard to make shoes for the poor. Nobody should be without shoes because they cannot afford it." The rabbi turned to God, *"Ribono shel olam,*

Master of the World. I am not worthy to sit with him."

The Talmud continues, *Kavata itim laTorah?* "Did you set aside a fixed time to study Torah?" Or, as the great sage Hillel taught, "Do not say 'when I have time I will study', because you will never have time."

There is a tale of a man who brought his son to a rabbi to teach him Torah. The rabbi asked, "Why do you want him to learn Torah?" "So that when he grows up, he will bring his son to learn Torah, and so on." The rabbi answered, "Better you should come and study Torah, so that when your son sees you, he will want to." We all send our children to religious school, but they rarely see us pick up a Jewish book, attend a Jewish class, learn a Jewish skill. Most of us have stopped our Jewish learning at age 13, about the time we begin to seriously explore every other subject. Then we wonder why our children lose interest after becoming a bar/bat mitzvah.

We need to put aside time to learn. I invite you to come study with me in my "Rap with the Rabbi," or the dozens of other classes and learning opportunities the synagogue offers. What is true of Torah study is true of every worthy endeavor. Do not say "when I have time I will exercise," because you will never have time. Do not say "when I have time I will go away for a weekend with my wife/husband, and work on our marriage," because you will never have time. Do not say "when I have time I will throw a ball with my son, play a game with my daughter, take my children out someplace fun, sit and read with them," because you will never have time.

The Talmud continues, *Asakta bepirya urviya?*

"Have you practiced the mitzvah of 'Be fruitful and multiply?" Have you brought children into the world? Most of us are blessed with children. But life is not fair, some of us are not so blessed.

The Torah gives us an out. According to the Talmud, anyone who raises someone else's child, or even teaches someone else's child, it is as if they gave birth to the child. You do not have to become pregnant or sire a baby to perform the mitzvah of "be fruitful and multiply." You just have to be a mentor. Teach a child. It could be your own, your grandchild, your neighbor's child, the children here at the synagogue. They need mentors, role models; our synagogue always needs volunteers to work with our children.

Finally, the Talmud asks, *Tzipita lishu'a?* "Did you look forward towards redemption?" Were you an optimist? Did you look forward to a brighter future? Do you remember the scene in "City Slickers" where Billy Crystal looks in the mirror and says, "This is the best I am going to look for the rest of my life!" It is all downhill from here. It was a fun movie, but even if Mr. Crystal is Jewish, that is not a Jewish way of looking at the world.

We Jews are the most optimistic of people. Who else but us, after the destructions and massacres and pogroms and Holocaust and evil, could take as our national anthem *Hatikvah*, The Hope. Who else could go to the death camps with Maimonides's words "I believe in the coming of the Messiah, and even if he tarries, every day I will wait for him to come." We will be asked, were you optimistic?

There is a story of a man who is stranded on a desert island. Every day he prays for rescue, but his prayers are never answered. He builds himself a shelter, and soon he has a comfortable home on the island. And he waits. One day, he knocks over the stove in his home on the island, and everything burns to the ground. He has hit rock bottom; he must start all over. Suddenly a boat pulls up. "We saw the smoke signal you sent, and thought that someone needs to be rescued."

On Yom Kippur we symbolically imagine our deaths. On Yom Kippur we think about the eulogy we will write for ourselves. These Talmudic teachings help us focus. Did we enjoy every legitimate pleasure God gave us to be enjoyed in this world? Were we honest in all of our business dealings? Did we set aside time to study, and for every other worthy endeavor? Were we fruitful, not simply by having children but by teaching our wisdom to a new generation? Were we optimistic, looking forward to a brighter future?

Each of us will someday be called to the next world. A judgment will take place. How will we answer these questions? What kind of eulogy will we write?

May Yom Kippur help us focus on what is truly important. And let us say AMEN.

Rabbi Michael Gold assumed the pulpit of Temple Beth Torah – Tamarac Jewish Center in Tamarac, Florida in 1990. Previously, he served as rabbi of Beth El Congregation in Pittsburgh PA, and Congregation Sons of

Israel in Upper Nyack NY. Rabbi Gold received his B.A. in mathematics from the University of California in San Diego. He was ordained by the Jewish Theological Seminary in 1979.

Rabbi Gold is the author of three books: And Hannah Wept: Infertility, Adoption, and the Jewish Couple and Does God Belong in the Bedroom? Both were published by The Jewish Publication Society. His newest book, God, Love, Sex, and Family: A Rabbi's Guide for Building Relationships That Last, was published in the summer of 1998 by Jason Aronson. Rabbi Gold's articles have appeared in Moment, Judaism, The Jewish Spectator, B'nai Brith International Jewish Monthly, and numerous other publications. He has lectured throughout the country on sexual ethics, infertility and adoption, and family relationships.

Through Heartfelt Communications, Rabbi Gold has released a series of audio tapes, "Family Through the Eyes of God." He writes a regular column for JewishFamily.com, an online magazine, and leads a weekly chat on America-on-Line. Rabbi Gold has served as the co-chair of the Rabbinical Assembly committee on sexuality. He can be reached through his website at http://www.heartfelt.com.

Rabbi Michael and Evelyn Gold are the parents of three children.

Forgiveness Coupons

Joel E. Soffin

---

*We need all the help we can get to build up
the courage for an act of true repentance.*

Years ago, when I was in college at SUNY Binghamton, we were given two choices of how we wanted to receive our grades. We could wait until all of the paperwork had been completed and receive everything in the mail some weeks later or we could write out postcards addressed to ourselves for each class. If we chose the postcard method, we would receive our grades much faster. That was the choice that I made, semester after semester, despite the fact that each time I would wonder why I continued to put myself into such an awkward and vulnerable situation.

You see, my father, *alav hashalom*, used to work in the post office. Now, although one is not supposed to read anyone else's mail — and I still refuse to open letters sent to other members of my family — despite this value of privacy, all of my father's co-workers would be on the look-out for those postcards with the big letter A or B written on them. When they found one, they would shout to each other: Hey, the kid got another A! Or, too bad only a B+ this time. Better get him to work harder next semester!

I was always the last one to know how I had done that year. Although I often denied it, the fact that everyone in the Long Beach post office knew my grades, did motivate me to do as well as I could.

I began thinking about postcards such as these when I read an article in the *New York Times* last June written by the columnist Maureen Dowd. "Vice President Gore," she wrote, "recently offered me a chance to repent. He sent me a Forgiveness Coupon." "(He really did)," she adds in parentheses. "The postcard-sized coupon reads, 'The Vice President of the United States hereby issues this Forgiveness Coupon to Maureen Dowd. We learn from our mistakes,' signed Al Gore (really)."

I was intrigued by this idea of a Forgiveness Coupon so I tried to contact Maureen Dowd in Washington to verify its existence. When I couldn't reach her, I called the Vice President's office directly. Although none of his aides were quite sure of what I was talking about, one of them agreed to research it for me.

He discovered that there were, in fact, such

Forgiveness Coupons, and the Vice President did send them out to a few people.

In sending one to Maureen Dowd, the Vice President was offering her a chance to win absolution, to be pardoned, for choosing to write a column that she knew would aggravate him.

My first thought on learning about these coupons was that they didn't seem very Jewish. As Jews, we cannot achieve forgiveness quite so easily. It takes more than just mailing a card to someone you've hurt or taken advantage of. There are several difficult and challenging stages that we have to go through before we deserve to feel forgiven. I hope that they will sound familiar to you.

In Hebrew, the word for repentance is *teshuvah*, which means literally "turning." The process of repenting requires that we turn away from the bad and harmful acts that we have been committing, that we re-orient ourselves and try to rediscover our ethical compass. We attempt to return to the place we were before such actions became part of our lives.

According to our tradition, this process involves several steps. First, we must admit what we have done. This may not be a simple thing to do, and it may take a long time to spell it all out so we can understand it fully. We must avoid rationalizing our behavior or finding excuses for it. Instead, we need to begin to take full responsibility for our actions.

That being done, we must demonstrate true remorse and regret for our behavior. It is not enough to speak to our family members and to our friends about how we would like to change. We also have to talk with those whom we have hurt or offended. As we read over and over again in our service: For transgressions against G-d, the Day of Atonement atones; but for transgressions of one human being against another, the Day of Atonement does not atone until they have made peace with one another.

So our regret and sorrow must be expressed directly to the people involved. And, we must offer to make restitution, to pay for any losses that may have been incurred.

Only then, can we ask for forgiveness. The process will be completed only when we find ourselves in a similar situation, acting properly.

This a long, hard ordeal. I wonder how many of us have succeeded in repenting in such a way even once during our lives?

How does this compare to simply mailing back a postcard? There is no real admission of any wrongdoing, no direct confrontation with the people who have been hurt, no offer of compensation and no way to say that you are sorry.

Yet, with all of this in mind, it still seems that the use of such Forgiveness Coupons can be very helpful to us and can be quite Jewish as well. We need all the help that we can get to build up the courage necessary for an act of true repentance, and these postcards may give us the courage to do so.

After all, when was the last time that you asked anyone to forgive you? When was the last time that you said you were sorry in anything other than an offhand way? And just as important, when was the last time you signaled to someone else that you were ready to forgive?

And so I'd like to look at these Forgiveness Coupons a little more closely with you. First, from the point of view of the person who gives them out. To whom would you send such a postcard? With whom would you want to preserve a special relationship even though there may have been difficult times between you in the past? To whom would you want to offer the hand of reconciliation before it is requested? Sending this postcard is not a sign that you expect bad things to happen again, but rather that should they happen you won't let them destroy your relationship.

Why would we want to act in this way? Part of the reason is that we have a need to forgive and to continue on with our lives. We want to maintain relationships with others even when they don't behave very well. We want to help them change back to behaving like the wonderful people we know and care about.

Many years ago I became estranged from my sister. Some very difficult things had happened in our family, and we stopped speaking to each other. It was clear to each of us that we were in the right and that we had been grievously wronged. It seemed as if the relationship was over.

Yet, after several years, my sister sent me what I chose to regard as the equivalent of this Forgiveness Coupon. Nothing was ever said openly; no statements of forgiveness or regret were made. Yet, somehow, we found a way to start again.

Neither of us wanted to be burdened with the pain of our past actions. We wanted to put those insults and hurt feelings aside. We tried to learn the lesson of the following rabbinic tale:

Two rabbis are on a pilgrimage to Jerusalem. As they are walking along, they come to a ford in the river. There they see a woman dressed in all of her finery. She didn't know what to do, for the river was high and she didn't want to ruin her clothes. Without a moment's hesitation, one of the rabbis took her on his back, carried her across the water and put her down on dry land.

The rabbis continued on their way. Soon, the second rabbi started complaining, "Surely it is not right to touch a woman; it is against the command-ments to have close contact with women. How could you violate all of these teachings?" On and on he kept attacking his fellow rabbi.

The first rabbi walked along silently until finally he remarked: "I set her down by the river, but you are still carrying her."

In the same way, we don't want to carry the burden of harshness and insults that we have experienced. We want to put them down, to leave them aside . Otherwise, they will continue to eat at us and to hurt us.

Yet, this does not mean that we have condoned what was said or done to us.

"What does it mean to forgive?" asks Rabbi Harold Kushner. "A woman in my congregation," he contin-ues, "comes to see me. She is a single mother, divorced, working to support herself and three young children. She says to me, 'Since my husband walked out on us, every month is a struggle to pay our bills. I have to tell my kids we have no money to go to the movies, while he's living it up with his new wife in another state. How can you tell me to forgive him?'"

Kushner answers her with these words: "I'm not asking you to forgive him because what he did was acceptable. It wasn't; it was mean and selfish. I'm asking you to forgive because he doesn't deserve the power to live in your head and turn you into a bitter, angry woman. I'd like to see him out of your life emotionally as completely as he is out of your life physically, but you keep holding on to him. You're not hurting him by holding on to your resentment, but you are hurting yourself."

So we need to send these Forgiveness Coupons to release ourselves from the angry emotions that can poison our lives, to give this ball of miserable feelings back to the person who created them, to release the control that they have over our lives. And hopefully, if possible, to find a way to become reconciled and friends once again. It's healthy, positive, and Jewish to be a forgiving person.

Perhaps this is the reason why it is taught that each night, before he went to sleep, Mar Zutra would grant forgiveness to everyone who may have done him injury.

Of course, there remains before us the question of how you can forgive someone who has not expressed remorse and has not asked in any way to be forgiven. Doesn't this just encourage people to do bad things to you, knowing that all you'll do is send them more and more Forgiveness Coupons? It still seems to let the other person off too easily.

Yet, there is even a basis for this unsolicited forgiveness in the Bible. When Job was suffering from all of the bad things that had happened to him and to his family, some of his friends came by to console him. They tried to find ways to justify the pain and suffering in his life. But what they said just made him more miserable. When at last God confronted Job directly and made it clear that his friends had spoken out of turn, it was God who told him to pray on their behalf that they might be forgiven — even though none of them had expressed any remorse or had asked him to pray for them.

The rabbis, based in part on Job's prayers, taught that if a person has received an injury, then, even if the wrongdoer has not asked his forgiveness, the receiver of the injury must nevertheless ask God to show him compassion. The ultimate reason for this teaching is that God is most compassionate to those who are compassionate toward others.

Still, one might think that such unearned forgiveness could have the effect of encouraging others to continue to hurt us and to behave badly toward us. So let us consider these Forgiveness Coupons from the point of view of the recipient. How will he react when he receives such a postcard?

The initial reaction may be one of surprise. Why would my friend or relative send such a coupon to me? What is it that she thinks I'm likely to do or do again that would disturb and upset her? What is it that I may have already done that bothered her? Right away, you would begin to review all of the interactions with her to discover what might have happened in the past. At the very least, your antennae will be raised to see your future actions in light of her willingness to forgive you in advance.

Many with whom I discussed these Forgiveness Coupons felt that the recipients would deal with them in a very cavalier way. Should I hurt you in some way, should I step on your feelings, I'll wait to see if you get upset. Then, before the situation explodes, I'll put this coupon in your face as if it were a "Get out of Jail Free" card in Monopoly and all will be forgiven.

I don't think that that's the way the postcards would be treated. I do not believe that our friends are nearly so callous or indifferent to our feelings. Rather, I believe that these cards can help us to create new and deeper relationships, ones in which it is possible to express disappointment and upset feelings and to offer forgiveness, ones in which such offers will be taken seriously and will lead to real changes in behavior.

If you were to receive such a coupon, what would it take to get you to send it back"

Just imagine that one of us were to mail back that postcard. Everyone in the post office, everyone in the recipient's family, would have the opportunity to see that we felt the need to be forgiven for something. That's a powerful thing, and to me it is a sign of sincere repentance. To send back a Forgiveness Coupon is to admit to having made a mistake; it is to show a desire to be forgiven.

Still, a stage of *teshuvah* seems to be missing. How can a Jew repent without acknowledging the specific thing that he or she did wrong? Don't we need to add a line or two so that can be spelled out?

I'm not sure this is necessary. When it has been returned to you, you will then be able to forgive your friend for every imagined slight or misdeed that she may have committed. You will be able to become a more forgiving person, less willing to hold onto old grievances.

I think that this is the message that the Vice President intended to convey to Maureen Dowd and I commend him for it. He knew full well that she would continue to write columns opposed to his position on various issues. His goal was to keep the lines of communication open, to remain colleagues who could still talk to each other despite their differences of opinion.

And, he wanted her to think twice before she punched hard at him in the future. I don't know if this will change the way Ms. Dowd writes, but I am sure that it will change the way in which we treat each other. We want, we need, to be forgiving people and we need to receive forgiveness.

Finally, what would the use of these Forgiveness Coupons do for us as a community? What would it mean for our synagogue and each of its families, to become specialists in giving and receiving forgiveness? How would our attitudes toward each other and toward the synagogue begin to change?

I think we would slowly begin to see each other differently. If we gave out Forgiveness Coupons instead of responding in anger when someone disappointed us or behaved badly, if we entered the building knowing that everyone here sought to behave in a kind and caring way and wanted to be forgiven when they failed to do so, the feeling tone would be remarkably different.

If every time we saw something wrong, something forgotten or overlooked, and we thought first about the need to forgive, then we might more readily offer to help, to repair what was lacking?

And even in those situations where deep feelings are hurt or where personalities clash, couldn't the exchange of these postcards help us to agree to disagree and yet enable us to walk on together?

If we could become a community of people eager to forgive others for their very human weaknesses and able to accept that forgiveness as being whole-hearted and real, then we would begin to touch each other's souls so deeply that the synagogue would become the true extended family we strive to be.

Think about all those people in your life, in your family, among your friends, the people with whom you used to be so close and to whom you hardly if ever speak, and give or send a forgiveness coupon to each of them.

Should you receive some of these cards yourselves, don't become angry or put off. Instead, reflect on your relationship and try to discover what it is that you might have done that would have been troubling or upsetting. Be thankful for the fact that the sender wants to reach out to you and to forgive you. Then, if you have the courage, if you have come to understand the purpose of these Ten Days of Repentance, send the card back. Who knows? Maybe a whole new relationship will begin.

I can almost see in my mind's eye hundreds of these New Year's cards passing among us, clearing the air and helping us to make the year 5759 one of blessing and friendship, of forgiveness and reconciliation. *Ken y'hi ratzon* — may this be God's will and our own.

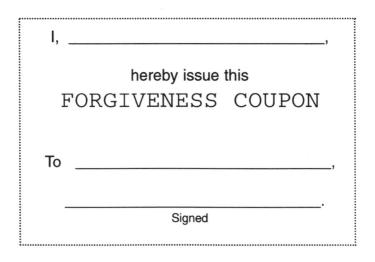

I, _____,

hereby issue this

FORGIVENESS COUPON

To _____,

_____.

Signed

Joel Soffin has been a rabbi at Temple Shalom of Succasunna, New Jersey, since 1979. Born in Brooklyn and ordained at Hebrew Union College, he has worked on a variety of social action projects both within his synagogue and on the national and international level. He has been published in Reform Judaism Today, Compass, *and has prepared Jewish Holidays and Social Action readers.*

Dancing Through Doorways: "The Binding of Isaac" and Contemporary Metaphors for Faith

Herman Asarnow

The story of the binding of Isaac is an external spur to our inward spiritual refinement.

When we conclude the Rosh Hashanah and Yom Kippur Holidays, the *yamim noraim* — Days of Awe — there is merit in confronting again perhaps the most troubling of the Torah portions we read at this time. "The Binding of Isaac" (Genesis, Chapter 22) is central to the very issue of Jewish belief and faith, what we try to renew in ourselves during these days. *Yamim noraim*: the root of *noraim* is the same as the word *yir'ah*, fear or awe. At the climax of the story, as Abraham is about to slay Isaac on the altar, the voice of God's angel stops him and says, "for now I know that you fear (or feel awe of) God." The Hebrew of the last phrase is *ki-y'ray elohim,* feeling awe of God. The text is telling us that, in offering up his beloved son Isaac, Abraham is inspired by the awe of God. And clearly, the story itself is meant to inspire such awe, *yir'ah* in us for God. Abraham had to confront God's terrible command-ment to sacrifice Isaac. And he went ahead with it, until stopped by God! We have to confront the ques-tion of what this difficult, hard-to-swallow story, repeated yearly at the center of our high holy days, tells us about our religion, ourselves, and the require-ments of faith. The Jewish liturgical calendar asks us during its most important spiritual week to confront this awe-full story. While for me this narrative is not literally true, I believe it contains that higher order of truth that stories embody — truth of feeling and spirit.

As must be true for many readers, my life is filled with difficult questions of faith — how can I believe in God? What is God to me? Who needs God? Only recently have I come in through the doorway of the synagogue myself. For a long time, I spent the High Holy Days at home, reading my prayerbook, alone. So it was not easy for me to walk into a sanctuary, stride to the *bimah,* and speak on these issues to a congregation of 600 fellow Jews.

What a struggle — all that I've learned in college, graduate school, and my late 20th-century life has led to a profound belief in the potential of human reason, faith in the continual advancement of humankind, a conviction about the central importance of the human, and not any kind of divine experience. Yes, even in the face of the Holocaust; perhaps because of it. Years ago, I found myself in agreement with such analyses of religion as those provided by Marx and Freud: religion is the opiate of the masses, and religious practice is simply a form of infantilism, psychological regression because of weakness of spirit that can't face the existential solitude of life. Yet recently, all this that permeates our intellectual climate, all that I've assimilated and believed through persistent study, has been struggling with something else in me that, ultimately, has responded both non-rationally and rationally to my Jewish traditions and liturgy as it takes wing in my *havurah* through passionate music, dance, argument, and community spirit — *ruach*. Still, I never could have willed myself through the doors at the back of our congregation's sanctuary and up to the bimah from which I first presented this *midrash*.

So how did I get through that door and up to that *bimah?* That's the question, and it parallels the question: How does Abraham let himself follow God's commandment to sacrifice Isaac? He was caught between his love for his son and his awe of God. I — and perhaps many of you — have been caught between our learning and reason and our desire to believe in God.

I have been drawn to the story of one hundred-year-old Abraham offering his much loved son as a sacrifice to God because, to me, above all else, it is a moving explanation of the difficulty of human belief, of the costs of spiritual faith. It is a story that I am proud to have as central to Judaism because it is frank, truthful, unromantic, plainly realistic about the seemingly impossible demands of spiritual life. The binding of Isaac is about the test that Abraham must undergo in order to understand what religious belief asks of us. The metaphor I find useful is to think of belief as a portal, a gate, a doorway, if you will, like the doorway in the back of every congregation's auditorium, which isn't easy to pass through, but which must be gotten through — repeatedly — if one is to be able to partake of religious life through our great tradition.

Let me tell you a story that illustrates what I mean by such a doorway, and that provides a metaphor for how we might get through them, and how Abraham may have seen his way through his.

This commentary on the binding of Isaac is about getting through doorways that seem barred to us but which we can get through, as did Abraham.

In years past, I have heard many useful and pained comments on Abraham's binding of Isaac. Most iterate a common response of repulsion to such a story that wickedly pits love against love, faith in God against the innate devotion we have to our children. For me, though, the binding of Isaac is about a test that Abraham participated in. The important word is in the very first line of the passage: "some time afterward, God put Abraham to the test." The key Hebrew word in the passage is *nisah* — to try, attempt, experiment, test. Its root is metallurgical, from the word that means "to refine." The Torah thus says that, after Abraham's sojourn in the land of the Philistines, God "tested" (so as to refine) Abraham by demanding that he offer up Isaac in sacrifice. As I see it, Abraham's *nisah*, his test in the story — and ours in reading the story — is allowing oneself to believe in God, despite such choices, or such stories, that don't seem logical or welcoming to our belief.

Abraham's challenge is to be willing to sacrifice what is most valuable to him in all the world — his son Isaac, conceived and born of his beloved Sarah in their old, old age. In fact, the great age of Abraham and Sarah is one of those details in the story that remind us it is a story of extremes in so many ways, a story about the very edge, the limits of human experience. Yet as parents — no matter how old or how long we waited to conceive our children — we can understand how having to sacrifice one's child is the very worst, the most extreme thing that could be asked of us. The horror of being the agent of our own children's death arises out of many things — the care we give them, their smallness, their reliance on us, but chiefly because our children are us, and are our future. Killing our children is a form of killing ourselves. The story of the binding of Isaac is about Abraham's willingness to sacrifice something of himself for the sake of his belief in something larger than himself, God. Similarly, Jews are challenged by the Torah to understand and perhaps even accept Abraham's decision, despite the fact that it goes against so much that we hold dear.

Belief represents a loss as well as a gain. If we are able to believe in a God that is infinitely greater in scope than we, we must give up the idea, the conviction, that we humans are the center of everything. The Biblical story asks Abraham to prepare to commit the most horrible, unreasonable act of self-destruction one can imagine.

A few years ago, in a speech given at the Jewish Theological Seminary, Christopher Lasch confronted the issue of our 20th-century disillusionment with religion — articulated by such great minds as Freud, Marx, Jung, and Weber, who all say that humankind has progressed past the need for religious belief. Lasch said that ours has been a too-prideful, too self-centered approach to life: "In the commentary on the modern spiritual predicament, religion is consistently treated as a source of intellectual and emotional security rather than as a challenge to complacency and pride... It is the belief that the purposes of the Almighty coincide with our purely human purposes — that religious faith requires us to renounce. Religion reminds us of the inescapable limits on human power and freedom."

It seems to me that the binding of Isaac is about how accepting belief in God requires a sacrifice, ultimately, of the primacy of self, and a sacrifice of reliance on reason alone as a guide to living. The story confronts us with a difficult truth, that belief in God exacts an almost impossible cost: we have to be in awe of God even more than in awe of our love of our children, or of ourselves. Abraham has to do nothing less than bind Isaac and place him on the woodpile, if he wants truly to believe, despite the fact that both his heart and his mind surely must have told him not to do it. The voice of God in the Torah almost "rubs it in" as it unnecessarily reminds Abraham in the second verse of the story to "take your son Isaac, your favored one, whom you love." And what parent can't imagine

Abraham's helpless, sick feelings when Isaac asks his father (verse 7), "...But where is the lamb for a burnt offering?" And I also can imagine Abraham's stomach twisting as he replies (verse 8), "God will see to the sheep for a burnt offering, my son." His feelings? Part faith, part hope, part anguish at lying.

The 11th-century Biblical commentator, Rashi, says that in this story God stresses the phrase "whom you love" to emphasize the extremity, and the enormity, of the sacrifice demanded and "in order to make very, very dear to...[Abraham] the forthcoming *mitzvah*" [which is both Abraham's amazing obedience and God's tender mercy] and "to give ...[Abraham] reward for every single weighty word of it."

What enables Abraham to obey the commandment of God? Judging from his whole story in the Torah, he certainly had spunk, energy, intelligence, and an independent sense of the world. But added to that he had the habit of ritual helping him along. Making burnt offerings was part of his religious ritual — as *davening*, singing, dancing, and even arguing continue to be part of Jewish tradition and much contemporary practice. Adding ritual, singing, and dancing to the capabilities of our reason gets our bodies moving when they are frozen stiff, when reason and will alone can't make them move. In part, Abraham was helped to achieve something higher by being able to go through the motions of ritual. To some extent, Abraham didn't have to will what he was doing. I contend that Abraham could never have brought himself to offer up Isaac if he hadn't offered up a thousand sacrifices before. His ritual helped him dance

through the doorway of belief, despite the great difficulty of doing so.

Is this a cruel, horrible story? Yes, and no. Yes
because even the mere thought of killing one's own
child is abhorrent, let alone having God ask us to do
it. No, because this Biblical story presents the idea of
a God that respects us enough to give us the facts
straight: that belief is the most difficult of all experiences. Its requirements are absolute. Abraham must
be prepared to sacrifice the child he wanted and now
loves more than anything — if he is to dance through
the doorway of belief. As the Torah expresses it (verse
12), experiencing "the binding of Isaac" is meant to
lead Abraham to experience *yir'ah* (the noun form of
y'ray) — fear or awe at the presence of God. For me,
at least, such awe represents the only presence of God
that I can experience; feeling the magnificence and
holiness of God gives me something to measure my
own small self against. All I seem at present to know
of God is this awe.

So how is the binding of Isaac relevant to us, 5000
years down the road? We don't have to sacrifice our
sons or daughters in order truly to believe. Instead,
we must at once value and yet also sacrifice the iron
grip of our worldly learning, our over-reliance on
reason alone, and our steadfast conviction that the
human experience is central — all of which can freeze
us in our spiritual tracks and keep us from dancing
through the doorway of belief in God. The story of the
binding of Isaac is not horrible, not ultimately cruel,
because of its happy ending, because Abraham does-
n't actually have to sacrifice Isaac. We really don't

have to abandon all that is good about our minds, our learning, our times, in order to believe in God or understand the story.

Life is large enough to contain both reason and belief, love of self (and progeny) in the same breath as love of whatever one understands as God. God bestows the blessing of innumerable offspring on Abraham — and us — in verse 18 — *shemata b'koli* — "that you have listened," because Abraham humbly chose to undergo this test and was refined by it.

A native of New Jersey, Herman Asarnow has lived for 20 years in Portland, Oregon, where, along with his wife, Susan, and children, Alison and Sam, he is a member of Havurah Shalom. Professor of English at University of Portland, he teaches poetry and Shakespeare. He is the author of poems and personal essays that have appeared in many magazines, including Beloit Poetry Journal, North Dakota Quarterly, High Plains Literary Review, Bridges, *and* The Seattle Review. *He also serves on the board of directors of Jewish Family & Child Service of Oregon, and has served on Havurah Shalom's Steering Committee.*

Where Are You?

Jeffrey K. Salkin

Imagine that the first thing you will hear in the next world is everything you have ever said in this world.

The Hasidic rebbe, Simcha Bunim, once went on a walk with his disciples. Along the way, he and his entourage encountered a group of Jews who were engaged in casual conversation. The rebbe said to his disciples, "Do you see those Jews over there? They're dead." The disciples were confused. Finally, one of them spoke up: "What do you mean, dead? They look perfectly alive to me." "They are dead," the rebbe said, "because they have stopped asking questions and searching for the right answers." The Hasidim walked on, pondering his statement. Finally, one of the bolder disciples approached the rebbe and asked, "Then, how do I know that I am not dead?" The rebbe turned to him and answered, "Because you asked."

The longer that I am a rabbi, the more I believe that the rebbe's answer to his disciple is our answer to ourselves. Why are we not dead, as a people? Why have we continued to live, even and especially in the face of brutal animosity, exile, homelessness, and physical and spiritual threats? Because we are the people that asks the questions and searches for the answers. It is an essential part of who we are as a people and as a religion. It is even part of our humor: "Why does a Jew answer a question with a question? And why shouldn't a Jew answer a question with a question?"

Judaism insists on asking questions that otherwise might go unasked — even if the answers are not readily apparent. We ask hard questions about existence and about ourselves. We are God's insomniac people: we lie awake in the middle of the night... we toss and turn when civilization is darkest... and we work tirelessly for the dawn. Rainer Maria Rilke put it this way: "Have patience with everything unresolved in your heart and try to love the questions themselves as if they were locked rooms or books written in a foreign language. Someday, without noticing it, you will live your way into the answer."

On these Days of Awe, 5759, I will be asking the oldest and the hardest questions that the world has ever confronted. They are the oldest because each one is from the Torah. Put them together, and you will have constructed a moral road map for the coming year, and for the coming years of your lives. The first question is the first question in the Torah, the first question that God asks anyone, the first question in history. This evening is the five thousand, seven hundred, and fifty-ninth anniversary of that question. It all happened on Rosh HaShanah: Adam was created; Eve was created; God placed them in the Garden of Eden; God commanded them not to eat of the Tree of Knowledge of Good and Evil; the servant seduced Eve into eating from the Tree; Eve shared its fruit with Adam.

"And the eyes of them both were opened, and they knew that they were naked; and they sewed leaves together, and made themselves garments. And they heard the voice of the Lord God walking in the garden in the cool of the day; and Adam and his wife hid themselves from the presence of the Lord God among the trees of the garden.

"And the Lord God called to Adam, and said to him, *Ayecha*/Where are you?"

"And he said, I heard your voice in the garden, and I was afraid, because I was naked; and I hid myself."

Ayecha/Where are you? It is the first question. It is the eternal question. I believe that it is the role of the Jewish people to ask that question of the world. As we stand on the cusp of a new century, I believe that it is our mission to America as well. The truth is that America is confronting a deep crisis. It is as bad as a financial crisis or as a military crisis. America is facing a crisis in the meaning of holiness. America has lost its sense of the holy. It is our role — we whose job description is to be an *am kadosh*, a holy people with a pedagogic mission to the world — it is our prophetic role to speak the truth to society. It is to ask the crucial question: *Ayecha*/Where are you?

What is God saying? God is saying *Ayecha!* We heard *Ayecha!* in the voice of an Orthodox Jewish senator from Connecticut, Joseph Lieberman. There are some who believe that faith should be private. There are some who believe that Judaism is what happens in these walls and in these books. There are some who believe that Judaism is something that only happens in the heart. But the synagogue has windows not only because we want to look at the trees. It has windows because we must see the world, and we must critique the world.

How proud I was of Joe Lieberman! In a religious climate that often seems (here comes my first bad pun of the year) like a non-prophet enterprise, he was our prophet Nathan, saying to our upgraded version of King David: "Thou art the man." "Mr. President," he said, "your behavior reinforces the worst messages of popular culture — that values are interchangeable. Mr. President, you have compromised your moral authority at a time when many Americans are trembling about the decline of the family."

That was Judaism saying "Where are you?" to the President. But what concerns me is not only what the President did with Monica Lewinsky, who is now (I say this with great sadness) the most famous Jewish woman in America. Enough said about that. It is what this scandal has done to our country. This is where we have truly lost our sense of holiness, and this is where we truly hear the cry, Where are you/*Ayecha*?

Let me take you back to the book of Genesis, back to the moment when Adam and Eve ate the fruit of the tree of knowledge. At that moment, they became conscious, and they were ashamed of their nakedness. How far we have traveled beyond the Gates of Eden. Rather than reaching for leaves, we moderns revel in revelation. There is that mythic sense of glee in seeing the emperor naked. Recall the Jewish version of that myth in which the sons of Noah see their drunken father uncovered in the tent, and are cursed for doing so. There is something within us that wants to see the father uncovered in the tent, and yet something within us wants to recoil in shame and in embarrassment. The daughter of Rabbi David Wolpe asked her father, "Are President Clinton's parents alive?" "They're dead, honey," he replied. "I bet he's glad," she said.

If anything sums up the mood of these Days of Awe, it is that observation of a young girl — that we have journeyed from the palace of our parents and we are not who we should be. The *midrash* suggests that when Potiphar's wife tried to seduce Joseph, he was actually about to do it, but at the last minute he saw his parents' faces before his eyes — and he lost his desire.

Let us ask ourselves what this entire matter teaches us. That is the Jewish way. The Clinton/Lewinsky affair teaches us what happens when we lose the holy. It teaches us what happens when we can no longer stand with the *havdalah* candle in hand and proclaim to the world that there is a distinction between the sacred and the profane. It teaches us what happens when we lose our personal boundaries, for there can be no holiness without them.

Someone actually suggested that Bill Clinton was a sacrificial offering for our generation. His affair teaches us what happens when we lose holiness in our relationships, when we sever intimacy from sexuality. It teaches us what happens when a society elevates the sordid over the sacred... when we dumb down our journalism to the level of supermarket tabloids. It teaches us what happens when we allow ourselves to become a nation of nudists and voyeurs. It teaches us what happens when we lose the holiness of language, when gossip replaces civilized discourse. This is where America needs our voice, and this is where it needs the voice of God: Where are you/*Ayecha!*

For, if America could turn to the Jews and say, "Teach us," what would we say? We would say that we have a value that we have always held precious. It is the value of *tzniyut*, of holy modesty. Orthodox Jewish women define that value as wearing high collars and long sleeves. But that's not the only kind of *tzniyut*. Modesty in dress and comportment implies that not all things are appropriate for public exposure or public discussion. Watching the news with our children has become a sudden mini-course in sex education. When the heathen prophet Balaam praised the Israelite dwellings and said, *Ma tovu ohalecha Yaakov*, how goodly are your tents, O Jacob, the *midrash* comments that Balaam had noticed that the tents were set up in a way so that the entrances of the tents did not face each other. Darwin said that human beings are the only creatures that blush — or that need to. We have forgotten how to blush.

Our liturgy speaks of the sins we commit *ba-galui uva-sater* — in public and in private. The distinction has evaporated. Once upon a time, it is written in Deuteronomy, the hidden things were left to God; now, there are no hidden things. Once upon a time, we called upon God as *Yodea Razim*, the One Who Knows Secrets. Now, there are no secrets (and listen to how close "secret" and "sacred" are to the ear). Once upon a time, the *Unetaneh Tokef* could speak of God as *Zocher Ha-Nishcachot*, the One Who Remembers All Things Forgotten; now, we, through our hubris, strive to usurp the Divine Mind.

A few years ago, in my last synagogue, Rabbi Eugene Borowitz was a scholar-in-residence. A local curmudgeon asked, "Why can't we say the unpronounceable four-letter name of God if we think we know how to pronounce it?" I will never forget Dr. Borowitz's rapier-like response: "Because we don't have to say everything we think we know."

That is a problem. For at a time when the body and the flesh begin to lose their boundaries, the tongue also knows no boundaries. We say everything we think we know, and we say a lot of things that we know we don't know. Look how many sins in our prayerbook refer to sins of the mouth. For the sin we have committed against you by gossip, and by talebearing, and by mocking and scoffing, and by falsehood, and by needlessly judging other people. In Hebrew, the sin of gossip is called *lashon hara*, the evil tongue. It is the subject of centuries of moral advice. Our sages, of blessed memory, wrote entire volumes about it. Entire *yeshivot* in Vilna and Slobodka existed where the curriculum was nothing but the laws of *lashon hara* — where the students became as expert in the laws of speaking as some were in the laws of slaughtering. *Lashon hara* means saying anything bad about anyone, even and especially if it's true. *Lashon hara* means insults, ridicule, and jest. *Lashon hara* means denigrating someone's possessions (never laugh at someone's car) or work or merchandise. It means commenting on someone's body or commenting on someone's mind or someone's money or someone's medical history. It means saying anything that might cause another person harm, embarrassment, or displeasure.

And why are we so obsessed about this? Because, as Rabbi Lawrence Kushner put it, we are not only what we eat, we are also what we see and say and hear. Language can be the most powerful thing in the world. Language has within it the power of life and death. To shame another person in public is tantamount to shedding blood. God created the world through language. The word *abracadabra* is Aramaic for "I shall create as I speak." What we say creates worlds. And what we say destroys worlds as well.

Where are you? asks God. Do you think that God doesn't know where we are? Of course God knows! God wants to know if *we* know where we are. In a world where holiness is slipping through our fingers, standing up for the holy is to search the darker places of the self. It is to acknowledge our weakness and our frailty and our shadows. It is to know that we are built of dueling urges, the *yetzer hara* and the *yezter hatov*, urges that let us descend to the level of the animals, and urges that allow us to ascend to the heights of the angels.

If we believe in a faith that says *Ayecha*/Where are you... then the voice comes from beyond and the voice is the voice of God. There is a God in the world. There is a God Who holds us accountable, and there is a God Who demands that we seek the holy in our lives. Our God judges us. And our God shuttles between the twin thrones of judgment and of mercy.

The *midrash* imagines that the cry of *ayecha* is really the beginning of the first exile — the exile from the Garden of Eden, the beginning of our loss of innocence. The *midrash* tells us that God created Adam as large as the world. But because of his sin, he shrank. The *midrash* imagines God speaking to Adam: How you have fallen! Yesterday you were ruled by My will, and now you are ruled by the will of the serpent. Yesterday you were the primordial being that extended from one end of the world to the other, and now you are small enough to hide among the trees of the Garden! Yesterday you were so large that you encompassed the world; now you have shrunken into yourself. You need to grow again and to reach again and to strive again. For this is the truth: When we sin, we shrink. We shrink into ourselves. Our world grows smaller. Our vision becomes narrower. But when we do *mitzvot*, we grow larger. We grow towards each other. We grow in our souls. We grow larger than we could have ever imagined.

To hear the voice of *Ayecha*/Where are you? in our own lives is to think about how we have shrunken in the past year — from the persons that we used to be to the persons we are now. And think about what it would mean to own up to it, and to grow once again.

The world needs our question. The world needs to learn from us how to ask the question of itself: *Ayecha?* Where are you? And the world needs our answer. There can only be one answer. *Hineni.* Here I am. Here we are. We are ready to speak to a waiting world again.

Rabbi Jeffrey Salkin is the senior rabbi of The Community Synagogue in Port Washington, NY. Born in New York, Rabbi Salkin was ordained at Hebrew Union College - Jewish Institute of Religion in 1981. He serves as a co-chair of the Outreach Commission of the Union of American Hebrew Congregations and is on the board of the Central Conference of American Rabbis. He earned a Doctorate of Ministry at the Princeton Theological Seminary, and has taught at the Hebrew Union College and the School of Sacred Music. His writings have appeared in such periodicals as The Wall Street Journal, The Jewish Forward, Reader's Digest, Moment, Reform Judaism, Newsday, *and* The Congressional Record.

Rabbi Salkin is best known as the author of Putting God on the Guest List: How to Reclaim the Spiritual Meaning of Your Child's Bar or Bat Mitzvah, *and* For Kids — Putting God on Your Guest List, *a version for young teenagers. He is also the author of* Being God's Partner: How to Find the Hidden Link Between Spirituality and Your Work. *His new book,* Searching for My Brothers, *which is about Jewish men's spirituality, will be published in the autumn by Putnam.*

Rabbi Salkin is married to Nina Rubin Salkin, a freelance writer, and is the father of two sons: Samuel, twelve, and Gabriel, six. He is an avid reader, loves movies, music, playing guitar, fiddling with computers, and vacationing in the Berkshires.

Choices That Matter

Carl M. Perkins

Trying to create the "perfect family" doesn't make our homes more loving or nurturing.

In the Talmud, in the first chapter of the tractate Berakhot, detailed instructions are given to couples who desire to determine the gender of their children.

Couples are told that if they wish, say, to conceive male children, they should orient their marital beds in a north/south direction, whereas, if they wish to conceive girls, they should orient their beds in an east/west direction. [*B.Berachot 5b*; Abba Benjamin, R. Hama b. R. Hanina, b'shem R. Isaac, based on Psalm xvii:14.]

Now, before anyone starts pulling out those old

Boy Scout compasses, let me say that in the almost two thousand years since that recommendation was made, I am aware of no evidence that it helps one bit. Put a bit more charitably, the technique probably works about fifty percent of the time.

And so it has been with the many other techniques that have been proposed. Nevertheless, that hasn't stopped people in every generation from trying to find a successful method of determining the gender of their children.

This age-old search took a promising turn recently. In an article published recently in *The New York Times* [September 9, 1998], researchers claim that they have discovered a new, highly effective method for determining the gender of a child at conception. For the first time in history, a gender selection technique that really works!

I applaud this new development, because whatever we learn about the human being can always be put to good use. The researchers are to be commended. Reproductive technologies, in particular, are extremely important. They have helped many, many couples conceive, which is a wonderful thing. And in the article, the researchers made clear that this new knowledge can help, say, couples at risk for passing on sex-linked genetic diseases, allowing them to conceive healthy babies when they otherwise might not be able to.

On the other hand, the researchers admit that they expect to be approached by many couples who simply prefer, for their own personal reasons, to conceive a child of a particular gender.

Now, I don't mean to pass judgment on those who might desire to do this. Who am I to say that, say, a mother of a dozen boys shouldn't try to shift the odds a bit to increase the chances that her next child will be a girl?

But if the desire to determine gender is just one part of a broader effort to try to create the perfect family, with just the right balance — which I suspect, in many cases, it is — then it is misplaced. It is futile.

Selecting a child's gender does not produce the perfect family. Human beings of both genders are, as we know, unique. Selecting a child with the "right" gender won't insure that they won't want a tongue ring or a tattoo; it won't make them more athletic or smart or hopeful or courageous.

The "perfect" family is, in any event, an idealized image, and trying to create it doesn't make our homes more loving or nurturing. Most important, determining the gender of our offspring does not protect us from what life may have in store for us.

In the liturgy that we'll be reciting tomorrow, there is a beautiful passage that, unfortunately, comes at a time when few of us are able to appreciate it. Many of us have gone home, and those that remain are generally weary. It is the prayer recited by the High Priest upon leaving the Holy of Holies at the very end of performing all of the rituals of atonement:

"May it be thy will," [the high priest says] "...that the forthcoming year shall be... a year of abundant prosperity, a year of grain, wine, and oil, a year of attainment and success; ... a year of enjoyable living; ... a year of success in business; a year of plenty and delight; ... a year in which you will bless the works of our hands."

And for the people of Sharon, a region that was subject to sudden earthquakes, he prayed: "May their homes not become their graves."

Why does the high priest recite such a prayer *after* he's performed all of the Yom Kippur rituals? After all, if he has been working all day at seeking atonement for the people, and has been successful, why does he even need to worry about these things?

The answer is that all the atonement in the world isn't going to put food on the table during tough economic times. All the atonement in the world isn't going to prevent illness or misery. All the atonement in the world is not going to prevent our homes from being torn down by a hurricane or destroyed by an earthquake.

The passages from the Torah that we read on Rosh Hashanah and Yom Kippur reinforce this. They expose us to the utter unpredictability of our lives and the impossibility of predicting our fates. If we had stopped reading Genesis at Chapter 19, would we have predicted (as we read on the first day of Rosh Hashanah) that Ishmael would have been banished from Abraham's home? Would we have predicted (as we read on the second day) that Isaac would have come so close to death?

Things don't always work out the way we plan. With austere understatement, the Yom Kippur Torah reading makes the point equally directly with its opening words, *"Aharei mot"*, "After the death...." Aaron, who is about to be instructed how to perform the rituals of atonement, has just suffered the loss of his two sons. We're not told exactly why, which is perhaps the point. How could any explanation ever be adequate to the existential challenge of explaining why bad things happen to us?

We don't know and we never will know what life will bring. We may reach a point where we'll know, as surely as we could ever know, that the gender of a child-to-be that we hope to conceive is female. But will we know whether she'll be happy? Whether, indeed, she'll be born at all, or live to marry and have children of her own?

Nonetheless, we actually have a great deal of influence over the future. In fact, we can determine the future to an unbelievable degree. The reason is that we are totally free to behave any way we wish. And we can choose to be good or to be bad.

The Talmud makes this explicit. In the Bible, there's a verse describing the creation of humanity that reads, *Vayeitzer ha-adam* — "And God created the human being." But the word *vayeitzer* is written in an unusual way, with two *yods* instead of one. Basing himself on this unusual spelling, Rabbi Yossi tells us that human beings are created with two *yetzers*, two inclinations; one toward the good and one toward the bad. And every one of us, not only Adam, is created this way. We're "hard-wired" to be able to make choices, to be able to act in different ways.

And if we make the wrong decisions, if we act improperly, we can always turn back. *Teshuvah*, repentance, is part of the structure of the universe. According to the rabbis, it was created before the physical universe. We can always turn back, from any path we've taken.

The choice at every moment is ours, and the outcome is ours.

A colleague of mine is the child of holocaust survivors. Her mother survived the war by living in a series of hideouts on farms in Poland. At any point they could have been detected, captured, killed. At one point, while they were hiding in a barn, my friend's grandmother insisted that my friend's mother, who was eight at the time, keep up her reading. Whenever food was delivered to the farmer who sheltered them, she would take the newspaper that the food was wrapped in and have the little girl read it to her. One of the others who was hiding with them yelled at her: "Why waste your breath? Why insist that the girl reads? What's the point? You should be putting all of your energy into teaching her how to survive!" To which the little girl's mother said, "Look, we're either going to survive or we won't. If we do, I want her to remember how to read." There's more to life than survival.

We may not have control over what happens to us, but we actually have enormous control over how we will respond. We have enormous control over what kind of people we are. Our challenge is to exercise that control.

A story in the Talmud teaches that at the moment of conception, an angel named Laila descends and scoops up the embryo and brings it up to God and asks God, "Will this baby grow up to be intelligent or foolish? Will it be strong or weak? Will it become wealthy or poor?" And presumably the angel gets an answer to these questions.

The text goes on to tell us, though, that there is one question that the angel does not ask: "Will this child grow up to become a *tzaddik* or a *rasha*, a good person, or an evil-doer?"

The angel doesn't ask this question because, even though God knows whether the child will become a boy or a girl and presumably knows the answers to all of those other questions, God doesn't know the answer to that question. God doesn't know whether or not any baby will grow up to become a *tzaddik* or a *rasha*. As Rashi puts it, in his commentary on this passage, "This is the question that God puts to us, for everything is in His hands except for this, which is in our hands." [*B.Niddah 17b, s.v. "Ki im l'yirah"*. See also *B.Berakhot 33b, B.Megillah 25a*] Whether or not we're going to do good is entirely up to us.

Let us focus our attention on what we can influence, which is how we will behave and how we will respond as we live our lives. May we worry less about what is beyond our control, and devote ourselves more fully to what is.

Rabbi Carl Perkins was born and raised in Philadelphia, PA. He attended Haverford College and received a master's degree in Talmud and rabbinics and rabbinical ordination at the Jewish Theological Seminary. Before becoming a rabbi, he attended Harvard Law School and practiced law for several years. Since 1991, he has been the rabbi of Temple Aliyah, a Conservative congregation in Needham, MA.

I Have Been One
Acquainted with the Night

Elyse Goldstein

---

*On his deathbed, Rabbi Zusya taught, "In
the coming world, they will not ask me,
why were you not Moses? They will only
ask me, why were you not Zusya?"*

I have been one acquainted with the night.
I have walked out in rain-and back in rain.
I have outwalked the furthest city light.
I have looked down the saddest city lane.
I have been one acquainted with the night.

(Robert Frost)

On March 30, 1993, the day after my birthday,
my only sibling, my sister Marsha, died unexpectedly. She was 40 years old. The last
conversation I had with her was the night before, and
the last words we exchanged were "I love you." There

has been a hole in my heart ever since. A baby is born and named after a loved one and the hole is not filled, only covered. It doesn't gape and it doesn't threaten, it just is. Only those with holes in their hearts know this, but we know it well, and its a sacred secret that we share.

I have been one acquainted with the night.

One week before Shavu'ot last May, one of my closest friends, Shira Shelly Duke, died of cancer. She was 41 years old. Many of you heard her speak last year on Kol Nidre, when she shared with us just how much all the many *misheberach* prayers through the years had meant to her. She told us that all those prayers felt somehow like the strings of a hammock being woven to hold her up, a hammock of prayers and *brachas* and poems and songs for her to lie upon and gaze heavenward. She stood on the *bima* and confided to us that although she prayed to be written in the book of life for one more year, she knew it was not long until the gates closed forever. And the hole is reopened and then re-covered once more.

Sometimes I feel angry and sometimes I feel confused but mostly I just feel lonely for them. So I do projects and give lectures and dedicate books but still: I have been one acquainted with the night.

People ask, which is worse? To know ahead of time or to be struck suddenly and unexpectedly. Which is worse? To die without meaning, to live without courage, never to have loved at all. Which is worse? To mourn alone, to wait in anxiety at a *shiva* house until the tenth Jew comes to make a *minyan*, to have no stories.

B'rosh hashana yikatavun, u'v'yom tzom kippur yeichateimun. On Rosh Hashana it is written, and on Yom Kippur it is sealed. How many will die and how many will be born? Who at a ripe old age and who before their time? Who by fire and who by water? Who by sword and who by beast?

It hurts so much to live in the face of death that even on Yom Kippur, even when we rehearse our own death by fasting and wearing shrouds and non-leather shoes, we want *unetaneh tokef* to be a metaphor. We want the inevitable question of who was here last year that isn't here now and who is here this year that won't be here next year to be a poem, or a parable. It's not. It's a wake-up call, it's a shofar blast of warning. No one knows when the gates will close forever so while we are inside them we had better love passionately, fight passionately, learn passionately, live passionately. *Unetaneh tokef kedushat hayom, ki hu nora v'ayom:* Let us declare the holiness of this day, because it contains an awful truth.

Awe-full. I'm filled with awe every day now. Every sunrise, every sunset. I say *shehecheyanu* a lot now: who has kept us alive, and sustained us, and helped us to reach this day. This day. *Unetaneh tokef kedushat hayom,* let us declare the holiness of this day, because it is the only day we have for sure. I love with urgency now. I fight with urgency now. I live with urgency now. I'm not waiting to have that anniversary party, I'm taking the kids to Disneyland when they are too young, I'm going to that family Bar Mitzvah in New York, I'm eating another chocolate.

Is there anyone here who is not one acquainted

with the night in some way? Some dream broken, some promise unfulfilled, some longing still agitating, some beauty just too far away to touch? There is a Zen parable about a woman who loses a child and goes to the master demanding that life be fair. "Go" the master says, "and bring me a mustard seed from a house that has never seen sorrow, and I will promise you a life of fairness." So she journeys from town to town and knocks on doors, searching for a family with no tale of woe. In this house she meets a starving child, in that one, a sick husband, in the next one, two brothers who have not spoken to each other in years, and in the next one, a bride and groom separated by war. She comes back to the master. "Have you found the mustard seed from the house that has never seen suffering?" he asks. "No" she says, "but I have found the gift of compassion."

On Rosh Hashana it is written, and on Yom Kippur it is sealed. But how we choose to live this year has not yet been recorded. With all our limitations, with all the choices not ours to make, still there is a way for us to chart the course of our lives. It's right there in the last lines, the crescendo of the *unetaneh tokef: U'teshuva, u'tefila, u'tzdakah ma'avirin et ro-ah hagezerah*: but repentance and prayer and deeds of righteousness help temper the severe decree. *Ma'avirin et ro-ah hagezerah.* These things temper the severity of the decree, but they do not annul the decree. The *gezerah*, the decree is set, and has been set for all time from all time. We all die. The gates close. But Judaism gives us a formula for loving what death can touch. *Teshuva* — reprioritizing and reconciling, *tefila* — prayer, and *tzedakah* — righteous deeds.

Life is a demanding teacher. I want to share the lessons I've learned so these three words, *teshuva, tefila,* and *tzedakah* will continue to be markers on the road with all its potholes and all its beauty.

Teshuva.

Reprioritize. When the gates close, there really are only a few people you can count on to shepherd you home. No one ever dies saying, "Gee, I wish I had spent more time at work." We say that our families are the most important things in the world to us, but we don't act like it. We say that we care about our health and our bodies, but we don't eat and sleep like we mean it. We say that we care about the quality of our inner lives, but we don't prioritize our spiritual needs as though this were so. It's not worth the extra hour at work to come home late again, miss story time again, too tired to make love again, too frazzled to think straight or read a book or take a class that you need for your self-preservation. And here's a secret we already know: "quality time" is a 90's advertising ploy. "Quality time" does not have to be in a foreign country, on a ski slope, in a cottage, on a cruise. Quality time is the dinner shared, the morning drop off, the evening bath for two, the early jog, the Shabbos candles moment. I never regret the times I'm just home with Baruch and the kids, the times I'm just sitting with my mom, the stolen mornings with friends. I only regret the times I could have, but didn't. We are so busy becoming the people we want to be that we are not enjoying the people that we are.

On his deathbed, Rabbi Zusya taught, "In the coming world, they will not ask me, why were you not Moses? They will only ask me, why were you not Zusya?"

When we are truly ready to reprioritize, we'll be ready to reconcile. That's what *teshuva* really is, turning around to face the people it's hardest to face. *Teshuva* literally means "turning" and it is done when we face the people we've put "behind" us. This is the time of year when we are supposed to ask if there isn't something in us that needs correcting as much as in the people we think need more correcting than we do. I never regret the times I said "I'm sorry" to my sister, only the times I didn't.

Tefila.

Why don't we pray with people in pain? You don't have to know the "right" words. Just close your eyes and ask them what they want to ask for. If someone you care about is depressed or anxious or hurting, either physically or emotionally, they need not only rational explanations but they also crave spiritual direction. And most importantly, they don't require a rabbi or a professional to "give" it to them; they need someone they trust to share it with them. How unfortunate that we leave the "religious" aspects of *bikur cholim*, of visiting the sick, to the clergy, to chaplains that have no relationship with the ill person outside of the hospital. We ask rabbis to "pray for" the people we love, but we feel awkward praying for them ourselves.

Spontaneous prayer comes hard to most Jews, yet the desire to say something remains. I'm sure you've all heard about the fact that prayer actually helps. Recently a test group of 300 patients in San Francisco were divided into two groups: those prayed for — even by strangers — and those not. The prayed-for group had lower statistical instances of the need antibiotics or second surgeries. I don't believe that saying a *misheberach* will cure a person of disease, but it often cures people of depression. And we get so mad at God when we've prayed for Grandma not to die but she does anyway. Prayer isn't magic. It doesn't take away death, but it often takes away despair. It's a hammock we weave for people to lie on and look heavenward. 1 never regret the times I prayed with Shelly, even when it seemed hokey. I only regret the times I didn't.

Tzedakah.

Jewish tradition teaches that every visit to the sick takes away 1/60 of the illness. We used to take *Shabbos* to Shelly in the hospital. Do you know those were some of our most wonderful *Shabboses?* We'd sing and all the nurses would come by; one week we forgot candles so we went down to the gift shop and it was around Christmas-time so we borrowed two of those electric Christmas candles with the artificial gold wax dripping down and we laughed all night about it. No, it wasn't always fun. Sometimes it was a big hassle, and the kids would act out and Shelly felt too sick to sing and it wasn't a Hallmark card event. Take *Shabbos* to someone in the hospital anyway. The whole thing — candles and wine and challah and kids if you have them. I never regret the times I visited, even the lousy ones. I only regret the times that I didn't.

And sometimes we'll have to visit the mourner. We Jews have lost the art — and I mean art — of shiva. You don't have to say anything clever, or spiritual, or religious. You don't have to answer the question "why?" and you don't have to ask it, either. You don't have to defend God or explain God. You just have to be quiet and helpful and confirm that they are still alive although their loved one is not. You just have to bring the coffee or run the errands or pick up the kids from school or make the *minyan* or sit for a while in sad silence and every now and then, offer a supportive sigh. Come during the day, when it's really lonely. If you're invited to stay for a meal, don't decline — they mean it when they say they want your company. The Talmud relates the custom that when someone died, the whole town would stop working when the funeral cortege passed by. Even today, I am deeply touched when I am in a funeral processional, and I see gentile workers on the street stand at attention, and take off their hats in respect to the passing cars. When it's us in the big black family car in the front — oh how we long for the world to stop and notice. Take your kids on *shiva* calls. It's not too sad for them. How will they ever learn by experience what it means to be a Jew who comforts the mourner? Even if time slips by and you didn't visit right away, don't worry. People mourn for a long time, not just for the first seven days. The card and the phone call both help the slow, aching, healing process. I never regret the times I paid a *shiva* call, only the times I didn't; even when it's tense or unbearably sad or even unbearably shallow.

U'teshuva, u'tefila, u'tzdakah ma'avirin et ro-ah hagez-erah: reconciliation, and prayer, and deeds of righteousness, help remind us that we aren't born alone, we don't live alone, and we won't die alone. I have been one acquainted with the night. But what gives me hope is that God is with me in the darkness, waiting to walk the saddest city lane right alongside. And though I've walked in the valley of the shadow, I have a road map to help me get out.

On Rosh Hashana it is written, and on Yom Kippur it is sealed. But how we choose to live this day, this hour, this moment — that has not yet been recorded. That is the signature of our own hand.

Rabbi Elyse Goldstein is the Rosh Yeshiva of Kolel: A Centre for Liberal Jewish Learning in Toronto and the author of ReVisions: Seeing Torah through a Feminist Lens *(Jewish Lights).*

Remember To Forget . . .
Learn To Forgive

Charles P. Sherman

More of us than we care to admit live in self-made dungeons behind bars erected by our own resentment.

We Jews have begun and will continue for the next ten days wishing each other and praying for a *shana tova*. May we all be inscribed and sealed for not a "happy" new year, but for a *shana tova* — a good new year. My sermons for these High Holy days tackle the question of what would guarantee a good new year? What can we do that would enable God to say: "You will have a good new year — I guarantee it!"

A Good Forgetery
My first suggestion may appear to almost run

counter to basic Judaism. We Jews are taught to remember — remember the Sabbath day to keep it holy. Remember Amalek. One of the key sections of the Rosh Hashanah morning service is *zichronot,* remembrances; and one of the most important services on Yom Kippur is *Yizkor* — may God remember. We Jews are taught to remember the Holocaust and to remember our covenant with God. Yet, strange as it may sound in several ways, I believe that a good "forgetery" is as essential to having a good new year as is a good memory.

I'm not sure that there is such a word as "forgetery" — let me tell you where I learned it. We recently watched the U. S. Open Tennis Tournament which was played in the Arthur Ashe Stadium. Arthur Ashe was a great tennis player who died much too young. Before he died he wrote a beautiful and inspiring letter to his daughter Camera. It was like an ethical will; Ashe tried to teach his daughter how to live after he was gone.

In that letter, Arthur Ashe tells the story of his premarital interview. He and his bride went to see the minister, one of the well-known leaders of the civil rights movement of the 1960s. After they met with the minister, they stopped to talk with his wife. Ashe said that the minister's wife gave him and his fiancée the best advice:

"If you want to make it in marriage, you need to have a good forgetery." By that she meant that you need to learn how to forget all the insults and the disagreements and the differences of opinion that you are bound to have at times in your life together.

Because if you don't, if you nurse every grudge, if you remember and wallow in every hurt, you will never have a decent marriage.

The Historical Spouse

I consider that extremely wise advice for husbands and wives. Someone once wrote: "Every time that we have a fight, my spouse gets historical." A friend thought he meant 'hysterical,' but he said: "No, I mean historical. She says to me, 'Do you remember what you did to me 10 years ago, and do you remember what you did to me 20 years ago?' Every time we have a fight, she gets historical."

In order to make it in marriage, you need to have not only a good memory but also a good "forgetery."

But this is true not only of husbands and wives; it is true in every arena of our lives. If we nurse our grudges, if we remember every slight we've ever received, friendship is impossible, parenting is impossible, life is impossible.

After What I Did to You?

I'd like to tell you two "forgetery" stories tonight from two different centuries — one modern and one ancient. Two different mentalities, contexts; but they both teach the same truth. The first comes from Rabbi Harold Kushner. When he was still a pulpit rabbi, Rabbi Kushner went to make a sick call on one of his hospitalized members. After they had exchanged a few pleasantries, Rabbi Kushner asked the man: "Would you like me to say a prayer with you?"

The man began to cry. Sobbing, he said: "You

would do that for me, after what I did to you?" Rabbi Kushner didn't know what he meant. "Don't you remember," said the patient, "the time when you came to the Board and made a proposal, and I spoke against it and it was shot down? And now you are willing to make a prayer for me after what I did to you?"

Rabbi Kushner says that it is not that he is such a great tzaddik; he had honestly forgotten the incident. But, think of that poor man who had been living so long with the belief that the Rabbi disliked him, the Rabbi was angry with him. How much better off he was that he had put it out of his mind; how lucky he was to have a good "forgetery".

The Best Way to Get Even

I read bumper stickers. I also read church bulletin boards. I think bumper stickers and church bulletin boards are often repositories of great wisdom. This summer in Tampa, when my wife and I were visiting with her mother, I read a church bulletin board that summarizes this important point: The best way to get even is to forget.

There is a cartoon of an elephant lying on a psychiatrist's couch, dabbing his eyes with a tissue, and the psychiatrist is telling him: "Of course I know you will never forget, but you need to work on forgiving." Many of us are that elephant. We can't forget; so we, too, need to work on forgiving.

How Can We Forgive?

How can we forgive those who insulted us, who hurt us, who wronged us in some way? Those whom we swore we would never talk to again, who never asked our forgiveness, maybe never even acknowledged their doing anything wrong? How do we rid ourselves of those grudges that are eating away at our *kishkas?* How do we forgive when we will never really forget what others did to us?

First of all, let's understand that forgiveness is the basis of these ten Days of Awe. If we can't forgive, why should we expect God to forgive us? All of us here know that at some time we've been guilty of angering and hurting another person. Some people no longer talk civilly to us because of something we did or didn't do — whether real or imagined. I know that there are people here who are upset with me. Sometimes my sense of humor has been misinterpreted as insensitivity, other times I've failed to meet a congregant's expectations, and sometimes I just haven't realized how I have offended someone. Winston Churchill once said: "Eating words has never given me indigestion."

I have failed. I am human. I have foibles, and I say to you tonight: if there is anyone here who feels wronged by me in any way — I beg you to call or visit with me during these next ten days and share with me your feelings. Give me the opportunity to make amends. I am asking you to forgive me. I hope you will regard this plea as if I were talking personally to you.

Like me, each of you may do things you are not aware of that others are upset with you about. That is why the rabbis suggest that, during these awesome days, we say to friends and relatives and co-workers

— if there is anything that I have done to wrong or to offend you, I ask your forgiveness.

Forgiveness is the courage to let go and to move on and not be trapped in the past. It is the power to project ourselves sympathetically, empathetically into the position of the offender. The French say "to understand all is to forgive all."

Forgiveness is the courage to see the whole person rather than to focus and fixate on the bad. Forgiveness is about remembering the kindnesses that someone did for us, not the errors they made. Forgiveness is the ability to understand that people change and mature.

To ignore the possibility that people can improve and develop is the essence of atheism. Humanity is made in the image of God, so to demean people and to deny this chance to change is to demean and deny God.

Moving Beyond the Hurt

Forgiveness begins when we move beyond the hurt. If someone hurts you, he doesn't also deserve the power to make you a bitter, resentful person, to change your personality for the worst. You don't get even by continuing to hurt, by seething with such rage that you can't enjoy the life you have. Get even by letting go, so that he can no longer pull your emotional strings. We must try to forget and forgive those things that — if remembered — bring out our most unworthy traits.

In a very interesting study, when people forgave another person and let go of a grievance they had been carrying around with them for some time — every single person felt a physical sense of relief, a feeling of having put down a burden.

During these ten Days of Awe we seek God's forgiveness for our own misdeeds. But we cannot solicit forgiveness unless we practice it. We cannot even believe that God forgives unless we can feel the power to do likewise. We cannot merit God's forgiveness for ourselves unless we are capable of extending it to others.

I Hereby Forgive

Let me offer you one suggestion on how we can let go of a grudge, how we can learn to put hurt behind us. This suggestion comes from Rabbi Isaac Luria, who in an all too brief lifetime founded the school of Jewish mysticism. Among the many things he did was to create a new prayerbook, one that is used to this very day by kabbalists.

In this prayerbook, Rabbi Luria introduced a new sentence. The daily evening service begins with a line from the Psalms: "In mercy, God forgives sin and destroys not . . . May God answer us on the day when we call." Rabbi Luria felt that he could not in good conscience say these words, that he could not ask God to forgive until and unless he was willing to forgive others. So, in his prayerbook, Rabbi Luria added this line to the service: "I hereby forgive whoever has hurt me this day." Then, and only then, could he say: "May God, in mercy, forgive sin and not destroy." Only when he had forgiven all those who had hurt him did he feel that he had the right to ask God to forgive him.

Let me suggest that we consider Rabbi Luria's line tonight. Try saying these simple words — "I hereby forgive whoever has hurt me this day." Not because the person who has hurt us deserves to be forgiven — maybe he does and maybe he doesn't; that is not the issue. But the person who has hurt us does not deserve the right to continue to hurt us. The person who has hurt us does not deserve the power to continue to have his misdeeds fester inside us and warp us. It is not good for the liver — in both senses of that word.

_____

A native of Pittsburgh, Rabbi Charles Sherman graduated from the University of Pittsburgh in 1963 with a B.A. in Philosophy. He was ordained by Hebrew Union College – Jewish Institute of Religion in 1969. He is currently the president of the National Conference of Community and Justice of the Tulsa Region. During his years in Tulsa, Rabbi Sherman has served as President of the Tulsa Ministerial Alliance, the Tulsa Police and the Fire Chaplaincy Corps, Tulsa Metropolitan Ministry, and the southwest Association of Reform Rabbis. In addition, he has served on the Institution Review Board of Hillcrest Medical Center, the Board of Directors of Leadership Tulsa, the Community Service Council, Planned Parenthood of Eastern Oklahoma and Western Arkansas, and the Policy Council of the Oklahoma Religious Coalition for Reproductive Choice.

Moving from Silence to Sharing:
A Re-Reading of the "Binding of Isaac"

Aaron Benjamin Bisno

What do we share of ourselves?
What do we choose to hide and why?

Istand before you this morning alone, hoping to share a thought, a musing, a reflection, that might carry any one of us into the new year with a sense of direction and purpose. It is an awesome task.

And it is one made more difficult for our not knowing each other well — if at all.

I am reminded of the 121st Psalm:

"I lift up my eyes unto the mountains; From where shall my help come?"

Who among us is not searching for direction?

Who can sit here and not feel the rhythms and mysteries of life reflected in the words and prayers we speak, echoed in the music and chants we have heard, resounding in the silences we share?

In spite of many years lived well, in spite of our educations and many-splendored life experiences, in spite of the love and security we know in the company of our closest friends and family, still there are times when it can feel as if our lives are without mooring; there are times when we may feel as if we are adrift and without certain direction

. . . From where shall our help come?!

The poet Ranier Maria Rilke suggests that we "be patient toward all that is unsolved in [our] heart[s]... [that we] try to love the questions themselves...." And then the poet goes on to insist that we "live the questions now, for [therein] we will gradually and perhaps without noticing it, live along some distant day into the answer." (Ranier Maria Rilke, *On Love*)

Let us see if we can "live along into the answer" this day.

We come together on this Rosh HaShanah morning, the first day of a new year, to rededicate ourselves to that which is most meaningful for us, irrespective of our station or calling, irrespective of our material wealth or yearning.

How do we move among others?

What do we share of ourselves?

What do we choose to hide and why?

It is on Rosh HaShanah morning — in these first moments of our year — that we are encouraged to ask ourselves these questions. It is here and now that we are challenged to explore sincerely and to share honestly our feelings, our desires, our longings, and our mortal failings. It is our task this day to take stock of our relationships, that we might better understand ourselves; that we might be better companions to one another.

This is not an easy undertaking. Sharing ourselves in a most personal way creates an intense and powerful experience. Sharing ourselves in such a way — even when we are alone with our thoughts — can be risky. To do so when others will see and hear us is all the more daunting.

For when we choose to share our inner feelings and thoughts, we must choose our listener carefully, for the one who hears us must be able to accept us wholly, with our failings. He or she must be ready to accept us even when we are most vulnerable.

If we are to be successful this Rosh HaShanah, then let us admit that each one of us seeks acceptance and love. We want to be understood, even as we are not exactly who we would like to be — this in spite of the personae and impressions we create for ourselves and for others.

This morning we heard the story of the *Akedah*, or the binding and would-be sacrifice of Isaac.

This story — of a father who, having heard God's voice, rises early one morning and under cover of darkness secretly spirits his son away with the intent to sacrifice him — is one of the most starkly vivid and arresting stories in all the Bible.

Widely interpreted, Jewish tradition has long held the story of the binding of Isaac to be a paradigm for faith. This morning, however, this Biblical narrative comes to teach us an altogether different lesson.

In the course of our story, we learn of a family's saga. Father Abraham, Mother Sarah, the boy Isaac — were each sorely in need of an opportunity to share their feelings. Each needed to talk and each needed to listen — and each missed the opportunity at every turn.

In spite of the story's familiarity, each time I read or hear it read I am overcome with sadness and melancholy. For, while intellectually I can appreciate the faith of which it speaks, as I listen to its words — and the silences between the words — I cannot help but feel the inconsolable loneliness of Abraham's spirit as he set off on his solitary task; I cannot help but imagine the fear that must have gripped Isaac's heart as he lay upon the altar. Consider the pain that ultimately claimed Sarah's soul as she awaited word of her husband and son.

God commands Abraham to sacrifice his son, Isaac. One imagines that upon hearing this command, Abraham must have been so overcome with dread, heartache and despair that, quite simply, it impaired his judgment. Could there be another explanation for Abraham not sharing what he believed God expected of him with his wife or with friends? Does he himself not even question it? Our text is silent.

Following the Divine decree, Abraham is rendered silent by his need to be strong, sure, and impregnable to weakness and uncertainty. He hides the most difficult challenge and task of his life from all those most dear to him.

And yet, where our text is silent with regard to Abraham's struggle and personal feelings, tradition records how Abraham covered his tracks.

In spite of the stoicism with which he approached his deeds, and managed to hide his actions, Abraham must have considered, "If I tell Sarah, she will forbid me to carry out God's plan. And yet, if I don't tell her, and am successful in stealing away with Isaac unnoticed, when she finds that we are missing... What then?"

It is quite clear that Abraham felt alone. He had no one to whom to turn and no one with whom he could share his grief. Abraham cut himself off from his wife, fearing for her emotional state and fearing that she might thwart his desperate plans. Neither was he able to speak honestly with his son. For even when the two journeyed, and Isaac asked, "Father, where is the lamb for the burnt offering?" Abraham dodged the question, answering obliquely that God would provide.

Abraham was not honest with his family and he was not honest with himself. He chose to share his feelings of sadness and guilt with no one — not even those with whom he was closest — and hence he suffered his loneliness in silence.

Although the story ends with Isaac being spared, it does not necessarily end on a happy note.

On their way up the mountain, father and son exchange banter and share conversation, and yet following Abraham's placing of Isaac on the altar, the two men never speak to one another again.

And the same is true of Abraham and Sarah. From the moment Abraham hears God's command and silently sets his mind to his task — in spite of the fears with which he was no doubt plagued — and then subsequently secrets his son away to be offered up to God, Abraham and Sarah never speak with one another again.

Having learned in this portion of her husband's emotional withdrawal and her son's imminent death, we can imagine that Sarah's death is initially emotional. We might say that the loneliness of silence killed her. For, in point of fact, in the portion immediately subsequent to this, we learn of Sarah's physical death.

Commentators have suggested that Sarah's death is tied directly to the distance created by the events in our story. What we can say for sure is that the strained relationship these three shared was exacerbated by their inability both to speak honestly and to listen to and for one another.

As he shared neither his inner thoughts, his heartaches, his anguish, nor his despair, Abraham suffered his loneliness in silence and it destroyed his family. He never knew again the company of his son nor his wife. For not having spoken from the heart with them when he could have, Abraham is denied the opportunity to ever share with them again.

So many of us know Abraham's pain. Who here has not been certain of the path we walk along? Who among us has not struggled alone with a difficult choice? Is there one here who has not suffered in silence?

But when we share the gift of our thoughts and our feelings with another, when we allow ourselves to cry on a friend's shoulder, when we express our innermost feelings with those we love, we forbid loneliness from bruising our soul. And we open ourselves to life's feeling.

And reciprocally, when we offer these gifts to another — a willingness to listen, a shoulder to cry on, a safe place in which one can unburden oneself, we perform an act of loving-kindness for which our tradition holds out the highest of praise. We have been taught that our world is sustained by such actions.

Our challenge this day, this year, is similar to that posed to Abraham so many years ago: to speak from our hearts.

Perhaps we fear we may be judged. Or perhaps we feel responsible for others. And we choose not to share our deepest selves for fear of how it may cause another to feel. Or perhaps we simply do not know how to share our feelings and our deepest selves. Whatever the reason, when we close ourselves off from others, when we disengage, we suffer and destroy the possibility of reaching that "distant day" of which the poet Rilke spoke.

And yet, withholding our feelings from those we care about is only half of the problem. The other half is not listening. Many of us would surely have to admit a weakness for gossip — we would have to admit enjoying "being in the know." Perhaps we shy away from someone wanting to share their innermost selves because we fear that we won't have the right answer, or worse, that this new confidant will expect us to share some of ourselves in return.

From where shall our help come, indeed?

It is not difficult to understand how it is that we may be without direction or mooring — even as we have been down this road many times before.

This morning's Torah portion began with Abraham being tested. The Hebrew read: "And it came to pass *after these things,* that God did test Abraham." Or translating the verse differently, but remaining true to the original Hebrew text: "And it came to pass after the words, that God did prove Abraham."

Perhaps this suggests that Abraham's was not a test of faith per se, but a test of whether Abraham could endure the pain of foregoing words — foregoing the ability to share his innermost thoughts and feelings with those for whom he cared most. Abraham may have passed the test of faith, but the test of relation — the test of words — he failed. And in that failing, his world was destroyed. Let this be our lesson.

The story of the binding of Isaac is the story of a family undermined by an inability to share. They did not talk to one another and they did not listen.

The story helps us to understand how imperative it is that we share our failures, our pain and our sorrow as well as our longings and our triumphs. It insists that we be honest with ourselves and seek what we need. And further, the story of the binding of Isaac underscores how essential it is that we listen for others' pain and that we do so with a caring ear and a kindred heart.

This morning begins a new year — a year of introspection and self-discovery. . .

And as we engage in this process of introspection,

taking stock of the ideal for which we aim, we must acknowledge that meaningful relationships require meaningful dialogue.

In the coming days, I invite you to take the risk of beginning to draw close to those around you; your spouses and partners, your parents and your children, your siblings and your friends.

And if you would say that you are already close with these people, then permit me to suggest that you risk sharing even more of yourself than they already know — it will give them permission to do the same. This coming week, dare to listen for others — both when they are speaking and when they are not speaking.

In this way, I believe, we will hasten the day that we will "live along into the answers."

(My thanks to Rabbi Richard M. Steinberg of Isaac M. Wise Temple, Cincinnati for his ideas, insights and constructive encouragement. This sermon would not have come to be had he not been there to help birth it.)

Rabbi Aaron Bisno received his B.A. in 1990 from Washington University in St. Louis, and his M.A. in Hebrew Letters in 1995 and rabbinic ordination in 1996 from the Hebrew Union College – Jewish Institute of Religion, Cincinnati.

During 1996–1998 Rabbi Bisno served as the Executive Director of the Hillel Jewish Center at the University of Virginia, Charlottesville. He is currently the Associate Rabbi at Congregation Rodeph Shalom in Philadelphia and Elkins Park, PA.

What Happens If We Never Meet?

Stephen S. Pearce

---

*Conflict between groups seems endless. Is
this what we Jews have to look forward to
as we enter the third millennium?*

Some years ago, when the British government was considering building the now completed tunnel to connect England with the continent, the budget office advertised for bids for the work. One bid submitted by the firm of Cohen and O'Brian was so extraordinarily low that a government representative was dispatched to see if the firm could do the work for the modest sum claimed. The office was on the fifth floor of a less-than-magnificent building in one of London's poorer neighborhoods. When asked if they could build a tunnel of such magnitude for such a small sum, Cohen replied, "Sure we can."

"But how can you afford to buy the equipment and hire the workers for so little money?" the representative inquired.

"What workers, what equipment? All we need is two shovels."

Taken aback by this response, the government representative asked, "How can you dig such a huge tunnel with just two shovels?"

O'Brian answered, "It's simple. I'll stand here and start digging; Cohen will stand on the continent and start digging. When we meet you'll have your tunnel."

"But what happens if you never meet?" the official insisted.

Replied Cohen, "Well, then, you'll have two tunnels."

We laugh at this story, but when we look beyond its humor, we find that it poses one of the most important questions Jews will have to ask themselves in the next millennium. In fact, it is the question that has defined Jewish life for the last two thousand years: What happens if we never meet? This dilemma is encapsulated in the old adage that says that when two Jews are stranded on a deserted island they build three synagogues — one for each of them and one that neither will set foot in. Deserted island Jews never meet. On this Yom Kippur, I ask you to consider whether we will we be any more successful than that.

Conflict in the Jewish community is not new, dating back to the Bible. Brothers — Cain and Abel, Ishmael and Isaac, Jacob and Esau, Joseph and his siblings, all endured powerful hostility and estrangement. They could not be civil to each other. They cheated, robbed, and even murdered, and this was among blood brothers. Think of the difficulty that unrelated clan members have had throughout history. Even Moses was not free of such strife. He endured several challenges to his leadership.

At the height of power, a rupture occurred in ancient Israel's monarchy following the reign of King Solomon that resulted in the split between the Southern Kingdom of Judea and the Northern Kingdom of Israel. In the years following the division, the relationship between the two kingdoms consisted of a series of conflicts and uneasy truces. The history of the period was written by historians of the Southern Kingdom of Judea simply because they outlasted the northerners. Thus, every northern king of Israel was described in denigrating terms. Conversely, every southern king was upstanding and righteous.

At the very beginning of the first millennium, the Saducees and Pharisees were at each other's throats over who had the right to determine what the correct forms and places of worship should be. While the Temple was still standing and operating under the rule of the priests, a new class of scholars known as rabbis established unauthorized worship communities called synagogues. Thrown into this equation were the influences of the upstart religion, Christianity, and various offshoots of Judaism and Christianity including the Essenes and the Samaritans. Thus, the foundation was laid for great conflict that is recorded in Jewish sources.

Even the Temple itself was believed to have been destroyed as a result of internecine conflict between Jewish factions of that period. The era of the creation of Talmud saw two competing Talmudic academies — one in Sura and one in Pumbedita — that vied for preeminence over Jewish learning in Babylon for over five centuries. It was anything but friendly competition. During the tenth, eleventh and twelfth centuries, the Karaites, who denied the legitimacy of rabbinic Judaism, became so powerful and confrontational that they were declared to be heretical and Jews were forbidden to worship with them.

One of the most fascinating conflicts between Jews was that of the newly formed hasidic movement of seventeenth century Eastern Europe that battled the established community of Jews called the *mitnagdim*. Led by the Gaon of Vilna, the *kahal* or community of *mitnagdim* officially excommunicated the entire *hasidic* population by the spring of 1772. Listen to the description of the then upstart community of *hasidim* by the *mitnagdim*, employing a play on words; the term *hasidim* or "pious ones" is substituted in this document of excommunication by a similar word, *hashudim*, which means "suspects."

> "...a sect of *hashudim*, suspects, meets together in separate groups and deviates in their prayers from the valid text...(In prayer), they interject obnoxious alien (Yiddish) words in a loud voice, conduct themselves like madmen...The study of the Torah is neglected by them entirely and they do not hesitate constantly to emphasize that one should devote oneself as little as possible to

learning, and not grieve too much over a sin committed. Every day is for them a holiday... When they pray according to falsified texts, they raise such a din that the walls quake... (We shall) extirpate, destroy, outlaw, and excommunicate them...they shall be torn up by the roots... Do not believe them even if they raise their voices to implore you for in their hearts are all seven horrors... So long as they do not make full atonement of their own accord, they should be scattered and driven away so that no two heretics remain together, for the disbanding of their association is a boon for the world."
(I. Cohen, *Vilna*, 1943)

This decree of excommunication, called *herem*, was the most powerful weapon that Jewish authorities possessed. Primarily used to maintain communal discipline, the excommunication ceremony — complete with the lighting of candles, the sounding of the ram's horn, and the recitation of formulaic prayers — was designed to strike terror into the hearts of dissidents and heretics and was the most grave action the Jewish community could take.

Conflict between groups seems endless: *Sephardim* and *Ashkenazim*, Litvaks and Galitizianers, and the Conservative, Reform, secular, and Orthodox conflict of today. Even among the various groups of *hasidim* there is enmity and suspicion. Is this what we Jews have to look forward to as we enter the third millennium? Conflict among Jews in Israel appears to be assuming more violent manifestations. The assassination of Prime Minister Yitzhak Rabin by a Jewish fanatic is the epitome of such extremism that is now present in modern Israel. The escalation of such divisions within Jewish life will not have a favorable outcome.

What happens if we never meet in the middle? We can look forward to more centuries of violence, bloodshed, and warfare among ourselves. If this is the example we set for the Jewish community, then you can just imagine how the rest of the world will view us.

In general, only during periods of national calamity — temple destructions, inquisitions, and pogroms — was there respite from such discord, although there have even been occasional moments when Jews obtained consensus during peaceful times. The best example is the post-World War II Jewish community that banded together to save the remnant of Jews who survived the Holocaust.

There must be a way to move away from the marginalization of those views we do not agree with, as the following anecdote illustrates. A rabbi was warned that his severest opponent, armed with powerful arguments, was coming to his home ready for a confrontation. When the adversary burst into the rabbi's home, full of absolute certainties, the rabbi raised his hand and uttered one word: "*efshar* — perhaps." He said, "*efshar* — perhaps you are right and I am wrong, or *efshar* — perhaps you are wrong and I am right." With that, the two men embraced and fell into earnest conversation. What happens when we never meet in the middle? We have to say "*efshar*" to those we have written off and discounted.

In spite of a long history of particularism that built walls between Jews, our tradition also has a deep appreciation of pluralism. Though sometimes it is a concept that is lost by fanatics, both ancient and modern, such genuine dialogue is well documented. The question is asked in the *Mishnah* about the value of recording the minority opinions of Hillel and Shammai, two rabbinic scholars who were frequently on opposite sides of an argument. It is recorded that they carefully reported the minority opinions of their deliberations in order "to teach the generations that come after, that none should unswervingly persist in his opinion, for even the greatest rabbinic masters were at times uncertain."

Pluralism in Judaism is not a new struggle. Rabbinic Judaism highlighted this problem by noting that when Moses received the Torah, he was also shown 49 possible ways that each law could be forbidden and 49 possible ways that each law could be permitted. (L. Ginzberg, *Legends of the Jews, Vol. 6*, 1959) This puzzling comment was intended to foster the notion that the interpretation of the law is entrusted to each generation of sages in order for them to render their decisions based on the different conditions of the times.

Do you remember how to hang a *mezuzah*? It is placed at a 45-degree angle on the right side of the door as you enter. This placement was the result of two opposing views. Shammai favored the horizontal position while Hillel favored the vertical position. They settled in the middle!

Arthur Waskow provides an elegant metaphor to help us understand the meaning of meeting in the middle. He suggests that the fringes on a prayer shawl serve as a buffer zone between the holiness of that spiritual garment and the rest of the profane world. It is the region where the spiritual garment melts away — where cloth and air are mixed.

To meet in the middle, there must be a middle, a buffer zone between where I end and you begin, where your property stops and mine starts. If a buffer zone existed between two hard-line positions, then Jews would have a common ground, a meeting place where they could speak of their differences with civility and not with angst and argument. The British historian Lord Acton said, "Every institution tends to perish by an excess of its own basic principle." That is the reality we face. If we cannot meet in the buffer zones of Jewish life, if Jews apply their own principles too rigorously, then the principles will not survive.

Twenty centuries ago, Hillel spoke words that have puzzled Jews for two millennia: "If I am not for myself, who will be for me? But if I am only for myself, what am I?" Hillel recognized the tension between self-interest and self-sacrifice, between being selfish and unselfish, obsequious and supercilious, humble and haughty. It is a delicate balance that serves as a challenge to Jews everywhere. Its foundation stone is centered on *efshar,* on the possibility of meeting in the middle, on genuine dialogue, on boundaries with fringes. Its keystone is the little-known blessing once regularly utilized by sages upon addressing a Jewish audience: "Blessed is He who discerns secrets, for the mind of each is different from the other, as the face of each is different from the other" *(Berachot 58a).* May this blessing serve as our compass when we dig tunnels toward one another, so that we may meet in the middle!

Stephen Pearce, PhD, is Senior Rabbi of Congregation Emanuel of San Francisco. He is the author of Flash of Insight: Metaphor and Narrative in Therapy, *and co-author of* Building Wisdom's House: A Book of Values for Our Time. *He is an adjunct faculty member at the University of San Francisco, a board member of the Pacific School of Graduate Psychology, president of the Northern California Board of Rabbis and columnist for the* Jewish Bulletin of Northern California.

Proposing an Alliance of the "3 Rs"

Jonathan H. Gerard

---

*Judaism has always believed that it is good
to be wealthy. Why? Because the wealthy
can do so much to help others.*

This morning I propose to go back to the year
1925 and change the course of American history.
I can only do it with your help.

Newsweek recently published a remarkable essay in
its "My Turn" column by an African-American scholar
— David Evans — who is an admissions officer at
Harvard University. Mr. Evans also tutors young
students at his black church in Boston's inner city — at
the Charles Street AME Church. One of the byprod-
ucts of his work is that he is "cursed" with recurring
anxieties about what is happening to a large number
of his people. The poverty and ignorance and despair

that plague so many young black people in our cities remain festering sores in both the soma and psyche of our democracy. Evans wants to do something about it. We should help him.

Now Evans is not really looking for our help. In fact, he really thinks that African-Americans should solve the problem. After all, many black Americans have risen to positions of prominence in our society in the past twenty years. And many others have risen to create a thriving black middle class. A black man has chaired the Joint Chiefs of Staff. Another has headed the Ford Foundation. Another has been a serious candidate for his party's presidential nomination. Evans points out that President Clinton has appointed more African- Americans to cabinet-level positions than had been appointed by all our previous presidents combined. Black TV show hosts and movie stars have changed the assumptions we make about the world we live in.

Yet for all this visible and palpable progress, for all the achievements of so many African-Americans in our life-time, there is, Evans points out, "a hidden tragedy." The recent runaway prosperity in America has taken place at the same time that the prison population in this country has also swelled. And the majority of our prisoners are black. More African-Americans go to prison than go to college. Although African-Americans compose 13% of the general population, 49% of inmates in state and federal prisons last year were African-American. And most of them were male. In 1995 fully one third of African-American men in their 20s were under criminal-justice supervision: in jail, in prison, on probation, or on parole. And in 1991, the year that apartheid ended in South Africa, the United States imprisoned four and a half times more black males per capita than South Africa.

Evans calls these figures "apocalyptic." "A generation of young black males is at risk," he says. If the trend continues, the majority of black American males will be what Arkansas educator Robert H. Martin describes as "doped up, locked up or covered up."

Evans calls upon the newly emerged black middle class to do something about this problem — but he addresses white America as well. The problem may directly affect the black community, but it indirectly affects us all. The costs of dealing with crime and maintaining courts, prisons, and rehabilitation programs is in the billions of dollars. We pay for it with our taxes. We pay for it with our loss of security. We pay for it spiritually as we mange to live comfortable, satisfying lives only when we turn away from the poverty and despair in those other neighborhoods.

Evans is not, however, a prophet of doom. He writes in order to propose a solution. And his solution is a very Jewish one. He looks to history to find destiny and there he finds a vast network of colleges and thousands of schools — built after the Civil War to educate former slaves. Former slaves established these schools, with the help of others — Andrew Carnegie, John D. Rockefeller, and Julius Rosenwald. (Julius Rosenwald? Who was Julius Rosenwald? ...I'll tell you in a moment.) Surely, recently liberated slaves who never had the chance to learn to read are very different from today's convicted criminals. But the threat they each pose to our society is, according to Evans, very similar. The schools that addressed this problem a century ago serve as a model for today. And for that reason, too, Evans's answer is also a Jewish answer. Our rabbis taught that of all the *mitzvot*, education is the most important, because it leads to the others. Evans also believes that an educated people will make a population of good citizens. (Yes, he perhaps has more faith than you or I — but for that reason alone he deserves our attention and admiration.)

Much of the success experienced by some members of the black community — from Colin Powell to Franklin Thomas to Jesse Jackson and Ron Brown and even Clarence Thomas — will become a mere footnote in history if affirmative action reversals continue to empty our schools of black students. Yet that is just what is happening. The University of Texas was closed to blacks in 1946 when Thurgood Marshall and others filed a suit that eventually integrated the Law School. But 50 years later the courts have outlawed the consideration of race by admissions officers at that same law school.

He looks out and sees that African-Americans have earned more doctorates in the field of education than in any other discipline. To this list he considers the skills of retired coaches and drill sergeants and wonders if such a consortium could join with corrections officers to bring something different into those prisons where thousands of new black Americans enter every month.

Blacks helping blacks. Blacks solving problems

through education. Who could object to it? Yet what does this have to do with us Jews? And on Rosh Hashana, no less?

What it has to do with us, on Rosh Hashana, goes back to Mr. Rosenwald. Julius Rosenwald, or "JR," as his descendants refer to him, was a Jewish business-man and philanthropist. He was born to German Jewish immigrants in Springfield, Illinois during the Civil War and, in the end, it may have been a book about slavery that had the greatest influence on his life. If I told you now what he did, you would simply not believe me. So allow me to prepare you a bit.

Rosenwald began his career working in his uncle's clothing store in New York City. During the six years he spent there he quickly learned what his uncle had to teach him about business, then opened his own store. Eventually he began manufacturing light-weight summer clothing, and in 1885 moved the business to Chicago, where it was very successful.

Meanwhile, another similar business had recently been established in Chicago — a small mail-order firm. Julius Rosenwald had an idea how to make this firm grow that was similar to his current manufactur-ing business. So he paid $37,500 to buy a one-quarter ownership in the establishment and become its vice-president. The name of the business? Sears, Roebuck and Company. In 1909 he was president. By 1925 his original investment of $37,000 had grown to a value of $150,000,000.

In addition to building the Sears empire, Rosenwald, who cared a great deal about his employ-ees, stressed recreational facilities and introduced a profit-sharing plan — both innovations that seem progressive even today.

But this is not a sermon on Jewish business successes. I am telling you about Julius Rosenwald because of what he did with his money. And because of what he can teach us. Rosenwald spent a fortune subsidizing the building of YMCAs for black Americans in 25 cities. From 1912 until the end of his life he served as a trustee of Tuskegee Institute. Closer to home, he gave $2,700,000 to build model housing for African Americans in Chicago. In 1917 Julius Rosenwald set up the Rosenwald Fund with a capital of $70,000,000. When he died, his will directed that all that money — principal and interest — be spent within 25 years. (This was twice the amount he left his own family.) Rosenwald also gave to Jewish charities, and served as President of the Associated Jewish Charities of Chicago in 1907.

Like Otto Kahn, Simon Guggenheim, and Albert Lasker, Julius Rosenwald was among those Central European Jews who, in the words of historian Howard Sachar, "turned almost instinctively to philanthropy as the appropriate expression of their gratitude to the American people." Yet no Jewish millionaire quite matched the record of Julius Rosenwald, either in munificence or sheer breadth of social compassion.

Rosenwald also read. And one of the most influential books to cross his probing gaze was Booker T. Washington's autobiography, *Up From Slavery*. After reading this book, Rosenwald became determined to do something to improve the quality of black education. He developed what he called a "seed-corn" approach. He offered to donate half the cost of a new school for blacks to any Southern community whose citizens would raise the other half. Can you guess how many "Rosenwald schools" were built? Rosenwald built 5,347 black schools and colleges! Private citizens and 883 county governments in 15 Southern states participated in Rosenwald's massive project.

What can we learn from Julius Rosenwald? Well, to begin with, we would do well simply to remember this titan of Jewish philanthropy. Judaism has always believed that it was good to be wealthy. Why? Because the wealthy can do so much more than the poor to help others.

But Rosenwald's example speaks to us loud and clear in the light of David Evans' plea in Newsweek. We Jews should be more sensitive to his call for help than anyone else.

And so this High Holiday season I say "let's do something." I propose that local Jewish federations and local NAACPs partner to build such schools again. Maybe in prisons, maybe in the inner cities. Maybe in conjunction with progressive schools of education at major universities. Rosenwald schools — all over America. Let the dialogue begin as to just how to implement this renewed partnership for the good.

In addition to the obvious social value of building these schools to solve the problem of our growing prison population, this proposal would, I believe, also achieve a number of other goals:

1. It would give direction and inspiration to a foundering NAACP, consistent with its historic mission. The NAACP has been wounded in recent years by scandal, by radicals, and by anti-semitism. Building Rosenwald schools in response to David Evans would recharge the organization with energy and purpose.

2. It would bring Jews back into partnership with African-Americans in the very locus of our original alliance (the NAACP). Many black Americans are vulnerable to the rantings of Louis Farrakhan. They do not see Jews who are sympathetic to the needs of the inner city or the ghetto. (Most do not even know that the very term "ghetto" come from the Jewish experience.) We live in different camps. Forging an alliance between Jewish Federations and the NAACP would bring an end to our overly long mutual isolation.

3. It would give a new and different vision to Federations, which are, like the NAACP (but for different reasons), foundering. This new vision would add to, rather than supplant, Federation's other historic and necessary goals.

4. It would bring a whole new generation of Jews under the Federation's roof — Jews who, for many different reasons, are not motivated by Federation's current situation. Money raised for this project would be new money — much of it coming from these new, baby boomers.

5. It would create a palpable answer to the hatred generated by Louis Farrakhan. Neither Jews nor Blacks know of Julius Rosenwald. Let's teach a new

"3-Rs" by building Rosenwald-Robeson-Rustin schools to address the special needs of those in prison or at risk of a criminal life.

Evans calls upon the newly educated black middle class to do this. But Jews, too, know something about education. And we, too, are struggling to find an answer to Louis Farrakhan, to bigotry, and to the continuing legacy of black suffering in America. Most of our families came to this land long after slavery was over. But that does not exempt us from "standing idly by the blood of our neighbors," whether they be black or Hispanic, or urban, or poor.

Two thousand years ago Rabbi Tarfon taught, "The day is short, and the task is great, and . . . the Master of the House is pressing." And he also taught, "You are not required to complete the work, but neither are you at liberty to abstain from it" *(Avot 2:20, 21).* If I initially took you back 75 years this morning, it was with the hope that the actions we take today for the sake of communal peace will make a difference in the lives of our grandchildren 75 years from now.

———————

Rabbi Jonathan Gerard was ordained at Hebrew Union College – Jewish Institute of Religion (NY) in 1976 and currently serves as rabbi of Temple Covenant of Peace in Easton, PA. He is a product of The Community Synagogue in Port Washington, NY (founding rabbi Eugene Borowitz) and one of five members of his religious school to become a rabbi. In 1990 he earned a doctorate in psychology and did his clinical training at the University of New Hampshire as a family therapist. He is indebted to Rabbi Louis Siegel, who most influenced his homiletics, to Rabbi Eugene Borowitz for his style of writing, to his father, Bert Gerard, and Rabbi David Saperstein, for his view of the centrality of social action, and to Rabbi Joel Soffin for his overall view of what synagogue programming should be. Rabbi Gerard is married to Pearl Rosenberg and has three children — Daniel, Rachel, and Sarah.

The Mezuzah:
Something to Reach for Every Day

Richard M. Litvak

The V'ahavta *within the* mezuzah
*reminds us that the Torah is our
not-so-little instruction book.*

Tonight begins a ten-day period of self-examination. As we pray together, hearing the voices of others around us, we are moved to lower the defenses that keep us locked into troublesome habitual patterns. We begin to be able to open the gates of our hearts and minds. We are led to honestly confess our flawed attitudes or actions. We allow ourselves to feel regret. We are encouraged to turn remorse into sincere apology and to repair the damage we may have done to others. Tonight, as we reflect on our lives, the truth is that most of the flaws we wrestle with are not major-league sins. They are the small transgressions that eat away at the quality of our relationships with others. At the heart of many of them is the problem of mismanaged anger.

Anger is a natural and fundamental aspect of life. Anger arises all the time, throughout the day. It signals danger or distress. However, there is only a single letter difference between the word anger and danger. To the degree that we express it poorly and fail to resolve it, anger spills out into our lives, with often dangerous, damaging consequences. Whatever sins we may be confessing during this season, many of them are a result of anger and its mismanagement. We withdraw. We pout. We nurse a grudge. We simmer and stew and blow our tops. We say harsh and nasty things. More often than not, it is our loved ones and friends who are injured by these angry actions.

In Judaism, we seek to achieve the spiritual goals of *shalom bayit,* peaceful relations in the home, and *darchei shalom,* peaceful relations in our daily lives in the world. Perhaps no ritual object and its traditions teach more about this quest than the *mezuzah* that adorns the doorposts and gates of our homes. Proof of this comes not only from tradition but also from the front page of a recent newspaper. What did Jewish astronaut David Wolf bring with him when he landed on the Mir space station? A *mezuzah.* Why? "The *Sh'ma* represents the oneness of God and all humanity," said the astronaut. It was the most important symbol he could think of for world peace.

I have heard about a family who threw away the inside of their *mezuzah.* They knew it had some important instructions, but the instructions were in Hebrew and they couldn't figure out what they were. The *mezuzah* is an untapped resource, right before us, filled with instructions about, among other things, how to manage anger and resolve conflict. Tonight I'd like to explore those instructions for harmonious living, which usually, literally fade into the woodwork, but are right before our eyes as we go out into the world each day and return to our families each night.

To begin with, the first thing we see when we look at a *mezuzah* is the Hebrew letter *shin*, embossed somewhere on the outer case. *Shin* is the first letter of *Shaddai*, the Hebrew name for God, and associated with strength. It is also the first letter in the Hebrew word for peace, *shalom*. It reminds us that God's presence is found where we are able to maintain harmonious relationships and that one of our highest spiritual strengths as human beings is the making of peace. Tradition bids us to reach up and touch it and kiss it as we come and go. In this way, everyday, we symbolically remind ourselves to desire to be at peace with others and to reach for this goal when we lie down and when we rise up, and when we walk by the way.

If the exterior cover literally impresses on us the goal of harmonious relations, the installation of the *mezuzah* suggests a way of pursuing peace. Rashi, the great Torah commentator, taught that the *mezuzah* should be vertical, perhaps to remind us that we are little lower than the angels. Then his grandson, Rebbenu Tam, ruled that it should be horizontal.

Perhaps this was to remind us that we are not God and therefore we should act with humility. What did the sages do? They decided to put it at a forty five-degree angle out of respect to both of them. So the posture of the *mezuzah* conveys to us that the world is filled with conflict within the home and outside of it. With Rashi, we must assert our values, openly and clearly respecting ourselves. But with Rabbenu Tam, we must also respect others and be humble enough to know that others have their needs and that we can be wrong as well as right. The resolution of this tension, as the sages suggest, is frequently through working out respectful compromises.

For instructions on how to do this, we now go inside the *mezuzah* to the scroll, where we find the *Sh'ma*. This prayer has so many meanings. We say it when we are fearful, to gather strength. It allows us to step outside the feelings and thoughts of the moment, to gain a different perspective. It is useful in dealing with another feeling, that of anger. When you look inside the scroll, the first thing you will notice is that the *ayin* at the end of the first word, *Sh'ma*, and the *dalet*, the last letter of the last word *echad*, are written larger than any of the other letters. They form the word *ayd*, which means witness. It is this one word that can rescue us at moments of anger or fear. We are asked to step back and *witness* our thoughts and feelings. Removing ourselves from the situation can help us to transform confrontation into respectful communication and conflict resolution. This ability to step back and disengage does not just happen. We have to nurture it and cultivate it on a daily basis, which explains the popularity of the best-selling volume entitled *Don't Sweat the Small Stuff; P.S. It's All Small Stuff*. This book gives us a variety of exercises to do daily, to help us practice seeing situations in new ways.

So too does the scroll give us similar instructions: You should experiment with loving with all your heart, all your soul, and all your might. You should keep the *mitzvot* of the Torah and its teachings upon your hearts." As we try to perform God's *mitzvot* in the way they are intended, we will gain new insights and develop new ways that help us to live more harmoniously with others, reminded daily by the *mezuzah* to keep these higher perspectives and ways of goodness on our minds. The result will be that our days will be good upon the earth. The *V'ahavta* within the scroll reminds us that the Torah is our not-so-little instruction book, and the *mitzvot* are the daily experiments that will help us live with greater harmony in our lives.

This helps us to avoid as much unnecessary conflict as possible. But when anger and conflict do inevitably surface, the *Sh'ma* and *V'ahavta* provide help. The etymology of the Hebrew word for compromise has three entirely different meanings. They form a three-fold program of cultivating our ability to move from anger to positive conflict resolution. (Rabbi Samuel Chiel, *Discovering Life's Meaning*, KTAV 1990, pp. 176–177.) The first meaning of this Hebrew word, *pashor*, is to cool down. The Talmud states, "Never try to appease a man in his anger." Anger is a powerful physiological event. It hijacks our thoughts and most other feelings. The first thing we often need to do is say the *Sh'ma* to ourselves. It will help us disengage and perhaps shift our stance from engagement to witness, from thinking only through our own perspective on the situation.

In the *V'ahavta*, the word *levavcha* is read by the Rabbis as plural, "your hearts." When we need to cool down, we can remind ourselves that there is a connection between body and mind, the emotional and physical heart. As we cool ourselves down, we remember that it is good for our own heart when we have a loving heart for others. There are actually several studies now that prove the wisdom of the traditional Jewish adage that we should have *rachmonus*, compassion. To calm ourselves down, and to have compassion for others, could help us live longer. I think I now understand what Rabbi Shlomo Carlebach meant when he taught, "If I had two hearts, I would have one for loving and one for hating. But since I only have one, I can't afford for it to be the one for hating."

The second meaning of the word for compromise, *pashor*, means to free one's self from old perceptions. I am reminded of the story of the man who goes to the psychiatrist because he is having a problem with his wife. He tells the psychiatrist that his wife treats him like a dog. "Well," said the doctor, "why don't you just lie down on the couch and tell me about it?" "Oh," said the man, "I'm not allowed on the couch." Sometimes, our worst fears and our sense of being treated unfairly, is real. Sometimes we just have a right to be angry and it is this anger that enables us to struggle for what we feel we need. But many times, we misinterpret what's happening, because we misinterpret from internal archaic perceptions that have kept us safe or satisfied before but become confining and detrimental. I recently read about a couple that exemplified this dynamic. The wife was chronically sloppy and her husband complained she regularly didn't put the cap on the toothpaste. She listened to this complaint and decided she would put the cap on that week. All week long she was disappointed her husband did not acknowledge her efforts. The next week she brought it up in their counseling session. Her husband responded that he noticed the cap was on and it made him wonder what was wrong that she had stopped brushing her teeth.

When we find ourselves frustrated or angry, it is hard to free ourselves of old perceptions. We say to ourselves: If they really cared they would have...I have a right to...It's unfair that...I would have done it for them...These are some of the thoughts that predictably arise. In the V'ahavta, we read not only that we have to love with all our heart, but also with all our soul, all our intellect and our highest level of understanding. It is not easy to notice and challenge old perceptions imposed on current facts. But we have to love with all our souls, to open our minds to new ways of understanding during points of conflict and impasse. The Kabbalah suggests that in every negative there is some positive. Often buried within a hurtful act is a good intention. Using all our intellect to reframe the conflict in this way, as an attempt at something good though flawed, can be one way to use higher understanding to turn the corner from anger to positive resolution.

Interestingly enough, this leads to the third meaning of the word for compromise, *pashor*, explanation. Sometimes we can free ourselves from previous perceptions when we seek explanations and understanding from another's point of view. Let me tell you about a conversation between two great commentators contained in the margins of the classic Torah with traditional commentary. (Rabbi Samuel Chiel, *The Gift of Life*, KTAV 1979, pp. 64–67.) The passage tells how Esau sold his birthright for some red porridge to his brother Isaac. Ibn Ezra, the great 12th-century medieval Spanish sage, offered this interpretation. "Esau sold his birthright because Isaac his father was so impoverished that there was no food in the house and he had to get food or starve." In the following century, the great sage Nachmanides offered a different opinion. He said that Esau sold his birthright to his brother because Esau was a hunter. He could be killed at any minute and might not live to see his inheritance. Nachmanides then adds, "I am amazed and I wonder how Ibn Ezra could have made such a stupid interpretation."

When you read further, you find that Ibn Ezra cryptically concludes with the words, *"Yesh lo sod."* "There is a secret in my commentary." What was his secret? Ibn Ezra was a fine Torah scholar but financially he was a very poor man. His son fell under the spell of a famous wealthy physician Hibat Allah. This physician converted to Islam, bringing Ibn Ezrah's son to convert to Islam as well. His son eventually converted back to Judaism before Ibn Ezra's death. However, you can imagine Ibn Ezra's sense of guilt that not providing materially for his son led, in a sense, to his selling his birthright. Nachmanides was, on the other hand, a wealthy man. When he went to settle in Israel, he left his son well off and in a fine position as the rabbi of his community. No wonder Nachmanides couldn't understand Ibn Ezra's commentary. He ridiculed him because he had no experience of what he had gone through. He had no idea of the sadness and pain behind his comments.

The third step in a more peaceful life is taking the time and making the effort to share and hear what is taking place in the heart and mind of one's self and another. The Talmud says in *Pirke Avot,* "Do not judge another until you stand in his place." It also tells us that both Hillel and Shammai, the two great sages, were honored. But Hillel's opinion was more honored because he always quoted Shammai's position first, before stating his own. Calming down, acting with compassion, opening up to see other ways of looking at something — all often find their fruition in sharing and understanding another person's needs and points of view and their understanding our needs and perspectives. Each of these in turn primes the situation for a caring and respectful resolution. Sometimes it will result in a heartfelt apology. Sometimes in a commitment to a change of behavior. Often it will develop into a respectful compromise.

Tonight we begin ten special days. We open the gates of change and growth and work together, until the closing of the gates at *Neilah* at the end of Yom

Kippur. It is true that after that, it will be harder to change, back on our own in our habitual patterns. But our religion also offers us the chance to grow every day. It gives us the *mezuzah* and its teachings on the gates and doorposts of our house every day of the year. If you don't have one, I encourage you to get one. If you have one, I hope you'll make use of it. Let it remind you to be the bearer of *shalom*. Emulate its posture of respectful assertion and humility. Let it remind you when conflicts arise that you can step back and be a witness, giving you control of your anger rather than being controlled by it. Fight for what you believe in and know what you deserve. But step back and cool down when things get hot. Remember, you'll live longer, especially if you culti-vate compassion as well. Exercise your freedom by allowing yourself to see things from different perspec-tives. Make the effort to explain. Most importantly, be like Hillel, who was known for peace, by listening and showing you can explain to another person their point of view. Reach for these high teachings and reconnect with them, as you reach to touch your *mezuzah*, going into the world and returning home to family and close friends. If you do, it will make managing anger and positive conflict resolution a slam-dunk in the new year.

Rabbi Richard M. Litvak has been the rabbi of Temple Beth El/Jewish Community Center in Aptos, CA, for 22 years. He graduated Phi Beta Kappa from Vassar College, major-ing in Religious Studies, and was a Hubbard Graduate Fellow in the Study of Religion. He received a Master of

Arts and Hebrew Letters and rabbinical ordination from Hebrew Union College – Jewish Institute of Religion. In *addition, Rabbi Litvak received a Master's degree in Counseling Psychotherapy from Santa Clara University and is a Licensed Marriage and Family Therapist.*

Rabbi Litvak serves on the Joint Commission on Religious Living of the Central Conference of American Rabbis and the Union of American Hebrew Congregations. Rabbi Litvak is published in several national periodicals, including the Journal of Reform Judaism *and* Reform Judaism.

Yizkor

Diane Cohen

---

*When we stand here at Yizkor, we must
remember that we are standing between two
generations: one that we remember, and one
that will remember us.*

The Yizkor service is clearly a service of remembrance. We bring warm, sometimes even painful memories to the sanctuary at this time of year, and we ask that God remember our loved ones for good and for peace.

We certainly don't need to be told to remember. Or do we? We are here, aren't we? What more could we possibly need to remember?

I read an article not long ago in an issue of the *World Jewish Congress Report,* an article on an event focusing on the Holocaust. A survivor was quoted as remembering a recurring incident. Repeatedly, he said when a fellow inmate of the camps knew he was about to die, he would clutch this man's hand and plead, "Don't forget me."

Those simple words moved me. First, the dying prisoners assumed that someone would survive to tell their stories, and so the account was a marvelous expression of hope in darkness. But those simple words said more. They seemed to say so much, and their message is true not only for the victims of the Nazis, but for all our loved ones who have left us.

What does it mean to say, "Don't forget me?" Don't forget that I existed. Don't wipe away all memory of me. My having been here has to have made some difference. Don't forget me.

Don't forget that you are here because of me. I gave you life. My love sustained you in dark times. You know how to love because of me. Don't forget me.

Some things are inevitable. I suffered. I had pain. I had doubts. I grieved. And I had triumphs and cheered my own achievements. All you are feeling I once felt. You learned how to respond to life from me. Don't forget me.

Don't forget what I tried to teach you. Don't forget what I stood for, what I cared about. My making a difference in this world is not just in buildings built or books written. It is knowing that you are keeping alive what I cared about. Don't forget me.

Don't forget that I too came from people who loved and cared for me. Remember that we are part of a chain that goes back generations, centuries, millennia. Remember where you came from. Don't forget me.

Don't forget I loved you.

But there is another subtext to "Don't forget me." Ultimately, don't forget I lived, and don't forget I died.

Remember that life is finite. That our days are numbered is not a fact to be mourned. It is simply a fact. It is less important to know how many days we have, than to know simply that our days are limited.

So now we come to a different kind of question. I once participated in a parlor game in which we were given questions of a moral nature and asked to respond. Of course, the questions became much more complex as we discussed as a group what the implications truly were.

One question was, "If you knew a nuclear bomb would drop in seven days, what would you do?" At first blush, some members of the group considered how to avoid the blast or protect themselves against a prolonged nuclear winter. Ultimately, however, we realized that "nuclear bomb" was a metaphor for the end of life on the planet. So the question really was, "If you knew life as we know it on earth would end in seven days, what would you do?" The responses, you will not be surprised to learn, became much more introspective. Parents, professionals, graduate students, all in their late 30s and early 40s, had to be confronted with the notion of their own mortality in a very immediate way. That is what Yizkor does, what the plea "Don't forget me" does. It reminds us that we do not have forever in which to move.

Let's allow ourselves more than seven days. I'd hate to have the world end during Sukkot! Let's say that we knew we had only 365 more days to live, that this is our last year. Would we do anything differently? I think our first reaction is to say, "Of course!" But just how would we change our lives? What would we do that we have not yet done? What would we no longer do? A recognition of our own mortality has a way of reordering our priorities. We all know of people who survived illness and traumatic accident to feel they were given a second chance, and who have responded with a dramatic change in their lifestyles.

What would you change? What would you make time for? What would suddenly become unimportant? I suspect these questions are a little discomforting, because there's something about Rosh Hashanah and Yom Kippur that transcends the other Yizkor recitations of the year. Anthropologists will talk about the need to mark beginnings and endings, and we stand at the beginning of a new year aware more than at other times of the passage of the months. We read the *un'taneh tokef* and are reminded yet again of the unpredictability of life. Perhaps we do have only 365 days. Who among us really knows? Perhaps a recognition of our mortality contributes to our tears as much as the longing for our loved ones.

As we recall our dear ones today, what all of us can share is the fact that they left us, as we will one day leave those who love us. It's not a fact to be mourned. It's simply a fact. So, will those we leave behind hear "Don't forget me?" And what will it mean to them? Don't forget me. Don't forget I existed. My being here has to have made a difference. Now is the time to be sure that our lives have counted for something. Don't forget you are here because of me. I gave you life. My love sustained you in dark times. You know how to love because of me. Be sure our loved ones know how we care for them — in deed as well as in word. Our children learn how to love from watching us.

I suffered. I had pain. I had doubts. I also triumphed. You learned how to respond to life from me. How do we respond to life? Do we see pain as part of the nature of living, or do we curse our lot? Do we acknowledge the Source of all good fortune, or do we take our blessings for granted? Are we teaching those around us how to respond?

Don't forget what I tried to teach you. Don't forget what I stood for. Do our loved ones know what is truly important to us? Do we support the institutions we believe in — Jewish communal institutions, museums, institutions that care for society's forgotten? Do we set examples by action of the importance of learning and caring? How will our loved ones know what we stood for?

Don't forget we are part of an ancient chain. Remember where you came from. Have we done all we can to teach that we are part of that chain? Do our loved ones know what it means to be part of the chain? Do they value it as much as we do? Don't forget I loved you. Don't forget to say it. If you wait too long, it might be day number 366.

When we stand here at Yizkor, it must be with the understanding that we are standing between two generations: one that we remember and one that will remember us. As our loved ones may have cried, "Don't forget me," let us resolve to do all we can today, so that we, too, will be remembered for good and for peace.

Rabbi Diane Cohen was ordained by the Jewish Theological Seminary of America in 1993. She holds a BA from UCLA in English Literature, an MA in Education from the University of Judaism, and an MA from the Seminary. She has published articles on prayer and Bible in Conservative Judaism *and* Jewish Bible Quarterly, *and in anthologies of women's prayers addressing pregnancy loss and Rosh Hodesh rituals. Rabbi Cohen has made contributions to the forthcoming* Humash *being produced by United Synagogue. She is currently at work on a book about Jewish prayer.*

Rabbi Cohen serves Temple Ohev Shalom, a Conservative congregation in Colonia, New Jersey. She is a member of the executive council of the New Jersey regional Rabbinical Assembly, and a member of the Middlesex County Human Resources Commission. She is one of the recipients of the 1999 Woman of Excellence award of the Middlesex County Commission on the Status of Women.

She is the mother of four children, Scott, Josh, Chuck, and Julie.

The Commandment to Love

Julie Schonfeld

---

*This is a Jewish theology of access, not a
theology of excellence.*

According to a certain tale, one morning in May,
two vacationers from New York, Tommy
Albright and Jeff Douglas, find themselves lost
in the forest of the Scottish Highlands. They wander
for hours with a useless map, which explains nothing
of the wilderness in which they have found themselves

Because they are lost and because they are scared,
they begin to talk about what is really on their minds.

Jeff is a pragmatist, a rationalist, a scientist. By his
own admission, he believes in only that which is
"real," anything he can touch, taste, hear, see, or smell.

Also by his own admission, he drinks too much, which is just fine with him. The last time he stopped drinking was at the urging of a wonderful girlfriend, only to discover when sober that they had nothing to talk about, and so broke up.

Tommy is an idealist, a believer in things he can't see. From appearances, everything is just what it ought to be in his life. He's got a great job, and is engaged to a wonderful woman — but something just isn't right. He has taken this trip to facilitate one of many postponements of his engagement

In the middle of nowhere, they spot a village that is not on their map. The place is quite peculiar — no phones, no cars. The villagers speak an arcane language they can't identify. And yet, the village is teeming with excitement. A fair is being held in the center of town. A wedding is scheduled for later that day. Every moment, it seems is pomp. Every footstep is pageant.

Tommy and Jeff are soon to discover what lies behind the charms of this place. They are told that a certain Minister Forsythe, loving his parish and worrying about the evils that might come from the outside world, had prayed that the town would vanish into the mists of the Scottish Highland to return only one day every hundred years.

This explained the arcane language and the intensity of the day's activity. Tommy and Jeff, one a cool rationalist, the other a passionate idealist, one of the head, the other of the heart, stumble into a single day of unlimited potential. In the words of the schoolteacher, Mr. Murdoch, "Welcome to Brigadoon."

In the next scenes, Tommy and Jeff begin to ask those questions so common to travelers who find themselves at a great remove from the everyday. What do I really mean by home? Tommy, like so many travelers, asked Mr. Murdoch: "Suppose a stranger to Brigadoon wanted to stay. Could he?" What would it be like to experience the intensity of this place, the closeness of its people, the strength of its passions, and the beauty of its pageant?

And what about this Brigadoon? This elaborate ritual, this ancient language. "Suppose a stranger to Brigadoon wanted to stay, could she?"

Mr. Murdoch's answer to Tommy is, of course, yes. And of course, in such a tale there is a condition, an obstacle to be overcome. A stranger can stay in Brigadoon, but only if he finds love there. Not just an onlooker's love, warns Mr. Murdock; an admiration for these committed people or this interesting place will not suffice. Love, an attachment that compels the deepest part of the self. Love, a shorthand, almost, for that which goes beyond the transitory moods of satisfaction and dissatisfaction.

In the musical, this love is the romantic Hollywood ideal — you can stay in Brigadoon if you fall in love with a person. But, if we are to extend this metaphor to Judaism, then finding love here must mean more than that. Love that we must find here, which would make us want to stay beyond one very occasional day, would require a very personal and a very powerful connection, which is both of the self and transcends the self.

It is the development of that kind of connection to

which I ultimately want to direct our attention.

It is worth noting, however, that in American Judaism, the Brigadoon metaphor is too true to life. The Hollywood romantic ideal carried the day. Relationship to Judaism, to the synagogue, certainly was defined by taking almost too literally the metaphoric equation that love between Israel and God is like love between two people. So, attachment to/engagement with Judaism has been reserved by and for weddings, *b'nai mitzvah*, and other life passages that call for caterers. Like Brigadoon, the synagogue was a place that emerged from the mist very rarely, but when it did, there was always a big show going on.

Cultural trends often eclipsed well-thought-out reconstructions of Jewish community and life cycle, and Jewish education ended rather than began with *bar/bat mitzvah*. Conversely, the ultimate cultural symbol for disengagement from Judaism was signified by and equated with intermarriage — people who found romantic love outside the community.

Back in Brigadoon, Minister Forsythe's solution created a few very troubling problems. The newcomer wishing to stay faced the obstacle of finding true love — but an even greater obstacle confronted people who were unhappy in the village. Minister Forsythe paid a high price in order to gain this privileged existence for his parishioners.

In the words of Mr. Murdoch, "If anyone of Brigadoon leaves, the enchantment is broken for all. That night, when the folks go to sleep, Brigadoon will disappear forever." For one person to leave was to bear the guilt for the destruction of the whole. Brigadoon depended on a unanimous avowal of devotion. Love of Brigadoon was not something sought and found. It was commanded of you and you relinquished it

In fact, the commandment to love is one of the earliest developments of Judaism. It is one of the fundamental innovations that takes place around the time of the destruction of the First Temple, 587 BCE. The commandment to love God, not as the result of a process, but as a pre-existing expectation, is a central aspect of the later development of the Bible. *V'ahavta* — and you will love the Lord your God with all your heart and all your might. This compulsion to love the Jewish God and express that love by remaining connected to the Jewish people was well supported by a long-standing historical agreement on the part of many other peoples of the world not to love us. Antisemitism facilitated the compulsion to stay. Where external supports for that compulsion broke down, beginning with emancipation and continuing over four generations in America, the spell was broken.

And, if the statistics offer even a grain of truth, people left in droves. With the frustration of people who believe deeply in what they say, but have no real power to enforce it, Jewish leaders, rabbis and parents began to deliver Minister Forsythe's message with ever-greater enthusiasm — "you should not leave, you cannot leave, please don't leave, why did you have to go?"

And, movie musical endings aside, the villagers pay a steep price. There is not only a wedding on that one day, but also the funeral of a broken-hearted man named Harry who tries to leave Brigadoon. The townspeople pursue him. Chased by a frenzied mob, he stumbles and dies of his injuries. Perhaps Harry is the person who came to Judaism looking for a home for his soul and found none, perhaps Harry is the person whose parents sat *shiva* for him when he took his searches elsewhere.

Fortunately, since the last generation, our communal discourse has modified its tactics to some extent. The Harrys of our community are no longer chased by a posse of loved ones shouting, "Come back or else." But even if we no longer use this rhetoric of life and death in order to blame those who become disengaged from their Judaism, we must nonetheless acknowledge that the very life, the vitality of our community hangs in the balance.

If, according to Jewish tradition, saving one life is the equivalent of saving the world, then surely preserving the relevance of Judaism for one Jew, is the equivalent of preserving Jewish civilization, the eternal bond, for all time. The same ought to apply to those presently not Jewish who genuinely seek a home for their soul here — either because they demonstrate a love for Judaism, or because they demonstrate a love for someone who is Jewish.

And yet the condition Mr. Murdoch placed before Tommy still dangles before our eyes. In order to take up residence in Brigadoon, in order to be a part of its reemergence in the next hundred years, the stranger must find love here, not just an onlooker's admiration, but something personal.

It is now almost a hundred years ago, in the community of the post-Enlightenment, post-emancipation liberal Jews of Europe, where this realization first came to the fore. To be Jewish in a free society, you had, it seemed, to choose it. Yet it is most curious that in that society of reformers and philosophers, one of its emblematic thinkers, Franz Rosenzweig, based his entire philosophy upon a reassertion of the *V'ahavta*, the commandment to love. It is this obligation to love that Franz Rosenzweig sets as the cornerstone of his post-emancipation theology.

Rosenzweig said, "Thou shalt love the Lord thy God with all thy heart and with all thy soul and with all thy might. Thou shalt love — what a paradox this embraces. Of course love cannot be commanded. No third party can command or extort it; the commandment to love can only proceed from the mouth of the lover."

Both love and command for Rosenzweig occur only in the context of a dynamic relationship. Commandedness is the momentum that moves the relationship forward. But how is this commandment, which can only issue from the mouth of the lover, to be heard? How is it acquired? Said another way, what are the Harrys of Brigadoon supposed to do?

This would be a good place to remember Rosenzweig's own Jewish journey. Raised as an assimilated German Jew, it was he who, in finalizing his plans to convert to Christianity, decided to do so in the most authentic manner of the earlier Christians. In order to highlight his intention to leave the religion of his birth, he decided to make a one-time visit to synagogue on the Yom Kippur before his baptism. That day, Rosenzweig renounced his plans to convert and spent the rest of his life studying and writing about Jewish philosophy and pioneering new methods for adult Jewish education.

In a series of essays called "It Is Time," Franz Rosenzweig laid the foundations for the maverick institution of adult learning in Frankfurt known as the Lehrhaus, which he founded with his colleagues Martin Buber, Erich Fromm, Gershom Scholem, and Nahum Glatzer. The Lehrhaus, which he ran from 1920 to 1929, became an influential model for numerous institutions of adult learning.

Rosenzweig wrote, "What we mean by Judaism, the Jewishness of the Jewish human being, is nothing that can be grasped as a religious literature or even a religious life. Nor can it be entered as one's creed in the civil registry of births, marriages, and deaths. The point is simply that it is no subject among other subjects. It is something inside the individual that makes [her] a Jew, something infinitesimally small, yet immeasurably large, her most impenetrable secret, yet evident in every gesture and every word — especially in the most spontaneous of them. The Jewishness I mean is not literature, it can be grasped through neither the writing nor the reading of books, it is only lived and perhaps not even that — one is it."

Rosenzweig's words are powerful, but their charge has, to a great extent, eluded us. One is it, but we still provide only a very few, very homogenous models for what it means to be it, to enact it, to perform it, to delight in it, to love it. To do it.

We are doing an excellent job addressing this challenge in our Hebrew school. Two years ago, believing that Judaism's deepest intent is the marriage of intellectual content and lived experience, we initiated a fully experiential Jewish afternoon school. We are committed to providing children with a learning experience that not only teaches them the basic skills of Jewish life and the foundations of Jewish thought, but also helps them develop their individual talents to create their own unique expression of Jewish identity. Our students learn Bible, prayers, holidays, ethics, and history, through multi-media, action-oriented activities such as drama, art, singing, movement and dance, building, puzzle-solving, and cooking.

So, in good Jewish fashion, we have done first for the children. What can we do for ourselves? How can adults engage in this Judaism of Rosenzweig where "one is it"? How can we hear the commandment to love proceeding from the mouth of the lover?

Everybody, at a minimum has at least the potential capacity to hear that voice. Even if you have never heard it in a Jewish language, so to speak. You may have heard it in a satisfying human relationship. Or, conversely in the growth process of coming to terms with rejection or loss. You may hear this voice in nature. Or you may have experienced this in your body. A sport where you tested your limitations and went much farther than you had ever gone. Or in a rare moment of real rest.

You achieved something you thought you couldn't. You were there when someone needed you. You fed someone who was hungry or protected someone who was in danger. You were a voice that spoke out so that people in need were not forgotten by people in power. You exercised human agency to good ends, you felt satisfied, and it stuck with you.

The list is infinite. At some time, you were carried along, even if only for a moment, on the wings of what we roughly call creativity, vitality, inspiration. It is a force by which life pushes itself along, bringing you along with it.

If you were born human, you have this capacity through no merit of your own whatsoever. This is a Jewish theology of access, not a theology of excellence, although it certainly leads to exceptional things.

You may not have encountered this capacity in what you associated with a Jewish context. It may never have occurred to you that through some gift you know you have or suspect you have, and which you enjoy using, you could encounter Judaism. Nor have you yet imagined that you may have the resources for love and support, engagement and vitality locked within this pre-existing, innate, Jewish part of yourself.

We are all villagers here in Brigadoon and we are blessed with an unparalleled resource. Judaism is a religion and it is also a civilization. All aspects of the life you live, the world you live in and the history from whence you come, are roads to enacting holiness and apprehending transcendence. If this Brigadoon had been on the map by which Jeff and Tommy navigated the forest, it would have shown countless roads to a life of meaning, connection, and purpose. It would have come with a compass — the direction of a loving voice that commands.

I would like to invite you to participate in an experiment. What would it be like if you engage these gifts that you have, these things you already know or suspect that you love, in a Jewish environment?

With the help of a Continuity Grant from UJA/Federation, our synagogue is initiating a pilot program called "Touchstones to Tablets." Touchstones, for our purposes, are those things in your life that inspire and renew you — particular hobbies, skills, talents, or relationships. In our brochure we say that a touchstone could be anything, from the art of painting to the art of parenting. We want you to encounter Judaism through those things.

The program is comprised of three one-hour classes, all committed to respecting people's many ways of learning. The first two are intended to provide the background framework that might be keeping you away if you don't feel like you ever got it. They are

1. Living Your Jewish Legacy — A Jewish Primer from a Civilization Point of View. This will get you started with the basics and expose you to Jewish ritual and Jewish theology as well as history and culture.

2. From Reading to Revelation — A Course in Basic Prayerbook Hebrew. The course is experiential. We will learn Hebrew through encountering Jewish prayer texts and learning to perform Jewish rituals.

3. Touchstones Seminar — An Incubator of Jewish Creativity. A research assistant and I will work with each participant in the seminar to design and

complete a year-long independent project — using that skill or talent you identify as a touchstone. A few examples: a project in Jewish calligraphy, a series of photographs dealing with the lives of Orthodox women, an oral history project on women who were leaders in volunteer organizations, a fiction project, an historical research project on Jewish views on adoption.

Too rarely has it been suggested that one of the standards by which the synagogue ought to judge itself is whether or not it provides an environment where the Jewish soul can pursue the small dreams as well as the big ones. Far too rarely has it been suggested that a synagogue ought to be a place where it is safe to take a risk.

Our work for today is not done, of course, until I tell you the Hollywood ending. Just as Franz Rosenzweig did on that Yom Kippur in 1913, Tommy, the dreamer, met Fiona, found love, and stayed in Brigadoon. Actually, first he went back to New York, where he discovered that he couldn't stay away from Brigadoon. He heard the voice of the lover who commands. What Tommy couldn't do for his New York fiancée, he had to do, he wanted to do for Fiona.

And as for the rest of us in our Brigadoon, in the words of Mr. Murdoch, "Sometimes I think I hear strange voices. They say no words I can remember. But their voices are filled with fearful longing. And often they seem to be calling for my attention. I've often pondered it and I think I have a feeling I'm hearing the outside world. There must be lots of folks out there who'd like a Brigadoon."

In 1987 Julie Schonfeld graduated Cum Laude from Yale with a BA in history and pursued a career in theater. Vying with her interest in the theater was a growing desire to explore her Jewish heritage. Although her grandfather was an orthodox rabbi, Julie Schonfeld grew up in a secular household. And, while her grandparents had emigrated to Israel at the time her parents married, books of jokes her grandfather used in sermons and reel-to-reel tapes of his exquisite cantorial voice were cherished possessions in the household. The road from public theater to public prayer became certain when Julie Schonfeld entered the rabbinical school at the Jewish Theological Seminary of America, where she is also pursuing a doctorate in midrash. Continuing to maintain her interest in theater, while in rabbinical school, she toured the US and Canada in an original one-woman show entitled, "Redemption and the Perfect Dress: So — You're a Female Rabbi, What's That Like?"

Shaming the Sinner

Marc Margolius

What kind of a tradition teaches that the Messiah will descend from a fatally flawed human being?

We hear a lot these days about personal redemption, which reflects the majority religious influence and American individualism. But in Jewish tradition, redemption is both personal and collective. Judaism teaches that one soul can't be saved while the rest of the world is going to hell. We've got to make it together. For us, bringing Messiah isn't a personal matter; it's a team effort.

Judaism describes a complex process of collective redemption; Jewish Messianism has numerous strands and is not easily described. But its basic structure goes something like this: first, the world was created whole; then it was broken; and in the future, it will be restored once more to wholeness. We can actually hear this process replicated in the notes of the *shofar*: *tekiah*, *shevarim*, *tekiah* — whole, broken, and whole. We live in the middle, in the fractured reality of human history, in the broken state of human imperfection. Our role as human beings is, with God's help, to fix the cracks within ourselves and within God's world.

The path to the Messianic future, the Jewish road to redemption, is paved with stories. They are not stories of superheroes or flawless characters. They are complex tales of human frailty, vulnerability, and deception, realistic stories of plain decency, simple acts of kindness and forgiveness. These stories teach us something about how we might redeem our broken selves and our broken world. I'd like us to address what our tradition has done with two of these stories, in the hope that they might cast some light on the situation in which we find ourselves today.

Our tradition teaches that the Messiah will descend from King David, a Biblical hero of outsized attributes and flaws. This is how the Book of Samuel describes the King's perhaps most famous and egregious sin:

> Late one afternoon, David rose from his couch and strolled on the roof of the royal palace; and from the roof he saw a woman bathing. The woman was very beautiful, and the king sent someone to make inquiries about the woman. He reported, "She is Bathsheba, daughter of Eliam and wife of Uriah the Hittite." David sent messen-

gers to fetch her; she came to him and he lay with her...
and she went back home. The woman conceived and she
sent word to David, "I am pregnant." Thereupon David
sent a message to Yoav [David's military chief of staff],
"Send Uriah the Hittite to me," and Yoav sent Uriah to
David.

In the morning, David wrote a letter to Yoav, which
he sent with Uriah. He wrote in the letter as follows:
"Place Uriah in the front line where the fighting is
fiercest; then fall back so he may be killed."

The messenger said to David, "Surely the men
prevailed against us, and came out to us into the field,
and we drove them back to the entrance of the gate.
Their archers shot from the wall upon your servants; and
some of the king's servants are dead, and your servant
Uriah the Hittite is dead also."

When Uriah's wife heard that her husband was dead,
she mourned for her husband. And when the mourning
period was past, David sent and fetched her to his house,
and she became his wife, and bore him a son.

Such is the story of David and Bathsheba. We have
to ask, What kind of tradition teaches that the Messiah
will descend from a fatally flawed human being capable of such wanton evil, a person who with impunity
commits rape and murder, a supposed leader who
repeatedly lies and uses his political power to perpe-
trate and cover-up his crimes? What redeeming
power is there in a story so graphically depicting
sexual misdeeds, a story that reveals such disturbing
truths about our political and moral role model that
we'd rather spare our kids the details?

Redemption emerges only in the larger unfolding

of this story. David's actions were evil in the eyes of God. So God sent the prophet Nathan, who confronted the king with a parable — in an indirect way, letting David see and acknowledge his crime.

"There were two men in one city; one was rich, the other was poor," Nathan told David. "The rich man had many flocks and herds; the poor man had nothing except one small lamb he had bought and nourished. The lamb grew up together with him and his children. It ate his food, drank from his cup, and slept with him; for the poor man, the lamb was like a daughter. Once a traveller came to visit the rich man, who was unwilling to prepare a meal from his own flocks and herds; instead, he took the poor man's lamb, and used that for the visitor's meal."

David became enraged and said to Nathan, "As the Lord lives, the man who has done this thing shall surely die; he shall restore the lamb fourfold, because he did this thing, and because he had no pity." Replied Nathan to David, "*Atah ha-ish,* you are that man. God says to you, 'I anointed you king over Israel, and delivered you from the hand of Saul; and gave you everything you wanted.... So why have you despised the commandment of the Lord, to do evil in his sight? You have killed Uriah, and have taken his wife to be yours. Therefore the sword shall never depart from your house; because you have despised me, and have taken the wife of Uriah the Hittite to be your wife. I will raise up evil against you from your own house, and I will take your wives before your eyes, and give them to your neighbor, and he shall lie with your wives in the sight of the sun. For you did it secretly; but I will do this thing before all Israel, and before the sun.'"

> David said to Nathan, "I have sinned against the
> Lord." And Nathan replied, "The Lord also has put
> away your sin; you shall not die. But because by this
> deed you have caused God's enemies to scoff, the child
> who is born to you shall surely die."

Confronted with his sin in a way that respects his
humanity and enables him to acknowledge his wrong,
David confesses, repents, and is punished. His illegit-
imate son dies and, for the remainder of his kingship,
his house is afflicted with internal strife and intrigue;
until his death, David knows no peace. Over the ages,
Jewish tradition has tended to idealize David and to
minimize his faults. But the fact remains that David is
a tragic figure whose misdeeds and achievements
remain public record for all time, whose flaws and
attributes are laid bare for all to see in every generation. The Bible hints that collective redemption is not
to be found in seeking perfection or in imitating idealized heroes. Redemption flows from acknowledging
human imperfection even in our leaders, and from
struggling to rise above it through repentance,
forgiveness, and change.

The redemptive process operates only in an atmosphere that acknowledges our fundamental human
frailty and that respects the sacred dimension of every
human life. On the one hand, we are mere flesh and
blood; on the other, we are created *b'tzelem Elohim,* in
the Divine Image. In addressing our moral failures,
we must take account of both truths. Therefore, the
Talmud teaches that "anyone who shames his fellow
in public, it is as if he sheds blood" [*BT Baba Metzia*

58b]. The sin of shaming another person publicly is described as *malbin panim* — literally, humiliating someone so openly and so thoroughly that the blood drains from their face. What's so terrible about shaming someone publicly? How can a sin involving only words be compared to murder? The Talmud illustrates the point with a story about the public treatment of King David after his sin had been exposed and he had repented *(BT Baba Metzia 59a):*

Rabbah ben Bar Hanah said in Rabbi Yochanan's name:

> It is better for man to sleep with a doubtful married woman [i.e., a woman whose divorce is legally uncertain] than that he should publicly shame his neighbor.
>
> From what source do we know this?
>
> From what Rava taught when he asked, What is meant by the verse: "But in my adversity they rejoiced and gathered themselves together... they tore me, and ceased not *(v'lo damu)."* [Psalm 35:15]

David exclaimed before the Holy One, "Sovereign of the Universe! You know full well that had they torn my flesh, my blood *(dami)* would not have poured forth to the earth. Moreover, when they are engaged in studying [the Talmudic tractates] *Nega'im* [ritual impurity conferred by leprosy] and *Ohalot* [ritual impurity conferred by tents stretched over a corpse] they jeer at me, saying 'David! What's the death penalty for one who sleeps with a married woman?' I reply to them, "He is executed by strangulation, yet has he a portion in the world to come. But one who shames one's neighbor in public has no portion in the world to come.'"

This text concerns the public treatment of a known sinner who has confessed — in this case, a sinner who also happens to be a public leader and whose sin involves sexual wrongdoing. And the teaching is clear and unambiguous — even in such a case, the public humiliation of such a sinner is unacceptable; it would be even worse than the crime that was committed. It is wrong to taunt or to ridicule in words or in deeds. Every human being, because of being made in God's image, has dignity and worth even if he or she has made a terrible mistake. Shaming another human being destroys their humanity in their own eyes and in the eyes of others — it ignores our inherent human fallibility and denies our inherent human worth. That's why the Talmud compares one who publicly shames with one who sheds blood; in each case, the aim is the destruction of a human life and the result is the diminution of God's image in the world.

Public humiliation not only destroys the wrong-doer's humanity — it pollutes the entire society. Shaming feeds the human tendency to focus on others' shortcomings instead of attending to our own. It fuels our voyeuristic instincts, and engages our potential for meanness and sadism. Above all, public shaming poisons the possibility of *teshuvah*, of honest confession, repentance, and change for all of us. Public shaming teaches us to conceal our faults and vulnerability from others and from ourselves.

Because this Talmudic passage involves King David, the personification of Messianism, we learn that public shaming is antithetical to the process of redemption. From this text, we learn that when wrongdoing is compounded by publicly shaming the wrongdoer, the Messiah is delayed. And from the rest of the passage, we learn that when wrongdoing is revealed and confronted with respect for human dignity, the Messianic era draws closer:

> Mar Zutra bar Toviah said in Rav's name — others say, Rabbi Hana bar Bizna said in the name of Rabbi Shimon Hasida — and others say, Rabbi Yochanan said on the authority of Rabbi Shimon bar Yochai: It is better to cast oneself into a fiery furnace than publicly put his neighbor to shame.
>
> How do we know this? — From Tamar. For it is written, "When she was brought forth, she sent to her father-in-law [etc]."

Tamar was the daughter in-law of Judah. She had been married to two of his sons, each of whom died, leaving her childless. Although Judah promised Tamar she could marry his only remaining son, Shelah, he never intended to fulfill that promise. Instead, Judah sent Tamar away to live in her father's house.

Many years later, Tamar heard that Judah was travelling nearby. Disguising herself as a prostitute, she sat by the roadside waiting for him. Seeing her but not recognizing her as his daughter-in-law Tamar, Judah engaged her services. Since he had no cash or animals as payment, as a security deposit he gave Tamar his personal seal, cord and staff — the ancient equivalent of his credit card. Later, when Judah tried to send his payment to the mysterious prostitute, she was nowhere to be found. "Let her keep the cord and seal and staff," Judah said, "lest I be shamed."

Subsequently, still unaware of the deception, Judah was told that his daughter-in-law Tamar had turned to prostitution and was pregnant as a result. Judah ordered Tamar to be burned, as the penalty for prostitution. But the Torah says and the Talmud quotes,

> "as she was being brought out [to be executed], she sent this message to her father-in-law: 'I am with child by the man to whom these belong. Examine them; whose seal and cord and staff are these?' Judah recognized them and said, 'Tzadka mimeini, she is more righteous than I, inasmuch as I did not give her to my son Shelah...' [Genesis 38:25-26]."

The R-rated story of Tamar and Judah is not one of those Bible stories we learned as children or we read to our kids. But it offers a Jewish model for the revelation and confession of sin. At the moment of truth, despite her grief and her outrage, despite the justice of her cause, Tamar privately gives Judah the opportunity to confess his wrongdoing, rather than accusing him publicly and putting him to shame. A midrash elaborates on the story, saying that Tamar threw the pledges before the judges with these words: "I am with child by the man who owns these — but I will not betray him, even if I perish in the flames. I hope that God will turn the man's heart, so that he will make confession" (Louis Ginzberg, Legends of the Jews,

Vol. II: 35–36).

Tamar's readiness to risk her own death rather than shame Judah in public prompts him to confess and to admit, *"Tzadka mimeini* — she is more righteous than I." Judah takes Tamar back into his home, never touches her again — and as a result of their illicit liaison, Tamar gives birth to Peretz, from whom David and the Messianic line descends. Thus begins the story of redemption.

Judah and King David each confess; each stands guilty as charged, and bears responsibility for his wrongs for all time. That the Messiah descends from them and from their immoral relationships reveals that redemption grows not from pretending to an imaginary standard of perfection, but rather from our ongoing struggle with our own inevitable human flaws. That the Messianic story begins with Tamar teaches that redemption takes root only in a society that protects human dignity and respects the holiness even of the wrongdoer. As Tamar demonstrates, redemption originates when, in our dealings with each other, we manage to temper *din*, the Divine attribute of justice and judgment, with *hesed*, the Divine quality of compassion and mercy.

As we begin a new year today, promising a fresh beginning for us all, may we rededicate ourselves to follow the example of Tamar: in judging ourselves, each other, and our leaders, we must stand on guard against the denigration of human worth. May we, of all people, not yield to the ever-present temptation to shame the sinner in our own lives, in our own community, and in our own nation. Nine days from now, at the end of Yom Kippur, we'll leave this space hearing the shofar's *tekiah g'dolah*. May we hear that long, unbroken note as God's voice, calling us this year to bring the Messiah closer by finally learning how to balance *din* with *hesed*, how to judge with compassion — how to act a little more godly, a little more humanely.

Rabbi Marc J. Margolius has served as religious leader of Congregation Beth Am Israel since 1989. A graduate of the Reconstructionist Rabbinical College and Yale Law School, he has served as co-chair of the Black–Jewish Coalition of Greater Philadelphia and is active in interfaith dialogue and social justice issues.

Yom Kippur and Death:
Have A Happy Death

Michelle Missaghieh

---

*Yom Kippur appears as a challenge to our
lazy and cowardly excuses.*

Malachy McCourt, in his best-seller book, *A Monk Swimming*, tells of a time when he picked up an old man on the road during a hard rainfall. When the man got out of the car he said, "Thank you, sir, for your kindness. May you have a happy death." McCourt said that his blessing echoed in his ears. He writes, "When you think about it, a happy death means you had a happy life. And I think I have... I've learned acceptance and letting go and to just keep a sense of humor about this absurd condition, which is that we are a species with a hundred percent mortality rate and not one of us accepts it."

(*New York Times*, "How a Rogue Turns Himself Into a Saint" July, 29, 1998.)

"A happy death." An odd phrase. Not the kind of thank-you one would expect. But death appears in all walks of life. Even our childhood fairy tales are chock-full of death. Cinderella, Hansel and Gretel, James and the Giant Peach, and Bambi all suffer the death of a parent. Amazing how despite our efforts to avoid addressing death's presence, our fairy tales remind us that none of us can escape our one-hundred percent mortality rate.

The Talmud reflects on our tendency to avoid confronting death with a story. As the soul of a great rabbi was travelling to the heavens, he told his students that even though death was as painless as taking a hair from a glass of milk, if God gave him the opportunity to go back to the world, he would never accept the offer, "because the dread of death is so great." (*Moed Katan 28a*). There are even stories of rabbis who try to elude death by engaging in superstitious actions: Rabbi Hanina ben Papa held onto a Torah scroll (*Ketubbot 77b*), Rabbi Eliezer ate holy food (*Moed Katan 28a*) and Rabbi Hisda sat on a bench and constantly recited words of Torah (*Makkot 10a*). But in the end the Angel of Death always got its way.

Why do we run away? Why is it so difficult to talk about our own end? Well, last year I asked you to think about the link between spirituality and your work — this year I'm aiming to make us all even more uncomfortable as I speak about death. Actually, our rabbis often compare Yom Kippur to the day of one's death. On Yom Kippur it's customary to refrain from life-affirming actions such as eating, bathing, dressing beautifully, and engaging in sex. In addition, on both Yom Kippur and just prior to death, Jews recite *Viddui*, a confessional prayer, in order to start our lives anew with a clean heart.

In the past year, I have been with many of you as you've faced your own mortality through illnesses, brushes with death, or mourning for a loved one. Sometimes I peer into a grave with as much confusion and anger as do you. I listen to your tears of sadness, guilt, anger, relief, and confusion. But even though we can't escape death, ironically many of us do not want to emotionally and spiritually prepare for our end. As a young newly-wed, I am just as guilty. I don't want to die now, because there are too many things I look forward to — growing in my marriage, raising children, traveling, reading, celebrating family *simchahs*, and the list could go on. And I imagine that no matter what your age — if you love life, there is always something to look forward to. The thing is, we never know when our time will be up. Nevertheless, we often use the excuse of endless tomorrows to avoid doing today's work around death, and, I would argue, around *teshuvah.*

Rabbi Joseph Soloveitchik, America's leading Orthodox teacher of the early 20th century, compared doing *teshuvah* (repentance) to mourning a death during *shiva*, because both the mourner and repentant seek forgiveness (*Man of Faith in the Modern World, Vol II,* pp. 125–132). By quoting Bar Kapara, he reminds us that a mourner is commanded to turn over his or her couches, beds, and mirrors. This ancient custom parallels the house's disarray to the messiness of the mourner's relationship with the deceased. Therefore the mourner is like a repentant who seeks forgiveness as a way of spiritually cleaning his relationship.

This year I met a woman whose brother died. For three days she remained silent. Finally when she did speak her words were loaded with pain and guilt. She told me how she was filled with deep-seated anger toward her brother, which he never knew about. Sadly, on the day of his death she even turned down his invitation to visit, just to hurt him. And now he was dead. His endless tomorrows ceased and she struggled silently in a messy search for forgiveness.

Rabbi Yitz Greenberg teaches that "the shock of death reminds us that time is too short to waste and too short to let pride and despair trap one in a life pattern with little in it to savor and respect." The awareness of death puts life into bold capital letters. Suddenly "no aspect of life can be taken for granted, (and) no feature of our (personality) is either eternal or absolutely necessary." (*The Jewish Way* by Irving Greenberg, pp. 200–203). But we're fighting an uphill battle, because the power of bad patterns is that they convince us that change is impossible; that our relationship with our sibling, spouse, friend, co-worker, is just ... the way it is. And now Yom Kippur appears as a challenge to our lazy and cowardly excuses. Today forces us to address our own mortality. It serves as a reminder that we don't have forever and that *teshuvah* *is* possible. Socrates once said, "The unexamined life is not worth living." Rabbi Greenberg reinterprets this Jewishly by saying, "To live the unexamined life is not really living," warning that, "if (we) are the same as (we) were last year, (we) have died a little in the interim." (ibid, reworded). In other words, a life without *teshuvah* leads to death, and Yom Kippur, the day of *teshuvah*, is our wake-up call to life.

It is not necessary to face your own mortality in the face of death. Denial is always an option. I have witnessed many families truncate *shiva* and scurry back to work because, "There's just too much to do." Sitting with pain is difficult, and that's what today is about. When we jump back to our routines, we miss out on the hard work of personal reflection and growth. We become threatened with a kind of psychic death in which habituation takes over.

The book of Ecclesiastes teaches "It is better to visit a house of mourning than a house of feasting; because (a house of mourning) is the end of all men and the living will take it to heart." (Kohelet 7:2). My husband jokes that since we've met, we've visited more hospitals than movie theaters. And it's probably true. I imagine that rabbis and emergency-room doctors confront death more that the average person. But even so, each of us can learn from Ecclesiastes. There is something very powerful about sitting with a family in mourning. Like on Yom Kippur, being with mourners puts my life in perspective. My priorities of family, health, love, communication, and kindness suddenly become crystal clear. My annoyances seem trivial and my personal flaws and family frictions glow with urgency.

I am reminded of one rebbe's teaching, that "True repentance brings joy" because, like death, it renews my zest and joy of life. Another irony. That's why Yom Kippur is sometimes considered a day of celebration, because when we look honestly at ourselves in the mirror, our denial dissipates, and suddenly we feel open, relieved, and joyful.

But to be open to true repentance, just like death, our lives must undergo a huge shift in self-awareness. The Talmud illustrates this shift in a series of death descriptions where the world undergoes drastic changes. When "Rabbi Abbahu died, the columns of Caesarea ran with tears. When Rabbi Jose died the roof gutters of Sepphoris ran with blood. And upon Rabbi Jacob (ben Acha)'s death, stars were visible during the daytime." *(Moed Katan 25b)*. These stories illustrate the violent, topsy-turvy, non-sensical feeling we experience with death and *teshuvah*. The Talmud even goes on to teach that once a person tears their clothing as a sign of mourning, he or she is not allowed to reseam the torn garment, thereby making it look like the rip never happened. But this again is uncomfortable. Covering up the wound and returning to status quo is so comforting.

Why put ourselves through the pain of realizing unfulfilled dreams? Why change our deep-seated ways? Why approach someone we hurt? Because we can. Because if we don't, we just might die a little. And because, as Clara Gordon, a 97-year-old member of our community told me last week, life gets better every day if only you work at it. If only we would listen to this woman's wisdom. If only we would allow ourselves to experience the urgency of life. Then what would our days look like? How would we treat our bodies? What would we say to our siblings? Parents? Children? Grandchildren? Neighbors? Co-workers? Friends? Do you see how joyful this could be?

Yom Kippur offers us that chance. We sit here today like mourners whose lives have been forever altered. Let's not hurry back home and metaphorically cut *shiva* short. Let's pledge to sit in community and turn over our couches, admit our weaknesses, and strive to live life with pride.

On his death-bed, Rabbi Eliezer was asked by his students, "When should a person engage in true repentance?" "The day before his death," whispered the rabbi. "But how are we to know when that day will be?" "Ah," said the rabbi, "that is why every day one must do *teshuvah.*"

Today is our day. May each of us have a happy death.

As a daughter of a Persian and a New Yorker, Rabbi Michelle Missaghieh has lived in two worlds. When she was in fourth grade she asked her parents why they didn't belong to a synagogue, and thus began her family's journey into the Jewish community. As a teenager she became involved with her synagogue youth group and received scholarships that supported her through many stages of her Jewish learning. She attended the University of Michigan in Ann Arbor where she graduated with honors in Women's Studies and Judaic Studies, and the Hebrew Union College - Jewish Institute of Religion, where she earned a Master's in Jewish Education in 1994. She was ordained as a Rabbi in 1996. She has worked at the Jewish Community Center on the Upper West Side in New York City and currently is the Associate Rabbi at Temple Israel of Hollywood in Los Angeles, where she lives with her husband Bruce Ellman.

Contributors to Living Words

Herman Asarnow
Rabbi Aaron Bisno
Rabbi Diane Cohen
Rabbi Shoshana Gelfand
Rabbi Jonathan Gerard
Rabbi Michael Gold
Rabbi Elyse Goldstein
Rabbi Richard Litvak
Rabbi Marc Margolius
Rabbi Michelle Missaghieh
Rabbi Stephen Pearce
Rabbi Carl Perkins
Rabbi Jeffrey Salkin
Rabbi Julie Schonfeld
Rabbi Joel E. Soffin

Selection Panel

Judy Bolton-Fasman
Rabbi Samuel Chiel
Rabbi Laura Geller
Rabbi Richard Israel
Rabbi Stuart Kelman
Rabbi Shaul Levenson
Rabbi Asher Lopatin
Rabbi Rachel Sabath
Rabbi Toba Spitzer
Rabbi Keith Stern
Rabbi Maggie Wenig
Dinah Zeltser
Rabbi Josh Zweiback

Contributing Editors of Sh'ma

Living Words: The Best High Holiday Sermons of 5760

Sh'ma is planning to publish Living Words each year, recording the issues of the year and the passions of the season. We would love to consider one of your sermons, either a sermon you delivered, or a sermon you heard, for inclusion in this collection.

Please complete the following form and return it to our office next fall with a "best" sermon of your choice.

Sermon Title:

Theme of Sermon:

Submitted by:
Name
Address (street, city, state, zip code)

Email
Telephone Number

I would also like to advance-order a copy of Living Words/Sermons of 5760 at the reduced cost of $11.95 (including shipping and handling).
Enclosed is $_____ for _____copies

Please send to:
Name
Address

Email

Return with check made payable to *Sh'ma*, to
P.O. Box 1019
Manchester, NY 03105-1019

SUBSCRIPTION INFORMATION

I WOULD LIKE TO SUBSCRIBE TO *SH'MA* FOR:

__ 2 YEARS AT $29   or   __ 1 YEAR AT $18

Name/Address:

Telephone:
Email Address:

Total enclosed: $_____

Subscribers may buy gift subscriptions to *Sh'ma* at a reduced price.

I WOULD LIKE TO SEND A GIFT SUBSCRIPTION TO *SH'MA* FOR:

__ 2 YEARS AT $20   or   __ 1 YEAR AT $12

TO (Name/Address):

Email Address:

FROM (Name/Address):

Total enclosed: $_____

Please mail, with check made payable to *Sh'ma*, to

P.O. Box 1019
Manchester, NH 03105

Jewish Family & Life!, the publisher of *Sh'ma*, also publishes these magazines on the Internet. Link your congregation's Website to these free on-line resources:

1. www.JewishFamily.com — the first family webzine for Jews of all denominations. This award-winning webzine is updated daily with articles and discussions that help families live Jewish lives.

2. www.JBooks.com — a source of reviews, articles and features about books and authors of interest to Jewish family members of all ages.

3. www.JewishHolidays.com — suggestions on how to turn a Jewish holiday into a meaningful family experience, including recipes, craft ideas, reviews of holiday-related books and music.

4. www.JewishCulture.com — commentary on and reviews of films, videos, plays, websites and radio programs.

5. www.JewishHealth.com — helpful articles on the wide gamut of health-related issues, from teen diabetes to stress — and all with a Jewish angle.

6. www.JVibe.com — a magazine for Jewish teens, with teen guest editors and writers, providing a Jewish connection for teens online.

7. www.InterfaithFamily.com — articles helping intermarried families cope with stressful issues, expert-moderated forums for these families, and resources, including programs offered throughout the world, as well as relevant books and films.

8. www.GenerationJ.com — a webzine for post-college pre-middle-age Jews who are starting out on their own and looking for support.

9. www.JFood.com — Recipes, cookbook reviews and holiday-related articles, all Kosher.

10. www.JTravel.com — articles on places of interest to Jews on vacation, as well as advice on how to travel successfully with your family.

11. www.AnswerAliza.com — provocative questions about religion and life as posed by an inquisitive five-year-old named Aliza. Responses are offered by people from around the world.